Taoist Ways to
TRANSFORM
STRESS INTO VITALITY

The Inner Smile
Six Healing Sounds

*I have come upon Master Chia's Taoist
practice in my old age and find it the most
satisfying and enriching practice of all
those I have encountered in a long life of
seeking and practicing.*

Felix Morrow, Publisher,
Healing Tao Books

Taoist Ways to TRANSFORM STRESS INTO VITALITY

The Inner Smile
Six Healing Sounds

Mantak Chia

AWAKEN HEALING ENERGY

HEALING TAO BOOKS/Huntington, New York

First published in 1985 by
Healing Tao Books
P.O. Box 1194
Huntington, NY 11743

ISBN: 0-935621-00-8
Library of Congress Card Number:
85-81656

Manufactured in the United States of America

Photographs by Richard Scott Duncan

SIXTH PRINTING, 1990

Contents

ACKNOWLEDGMENTS

I thank foremost those Taoist Masters who were kind enough to share their knowledge with me, never imagining it would eventually be taught to Westerners. I acknowledge special thanks to Dena Saxer for seeing the need for this book to be published and for her encouragement and hard work on the initial manuscript.

I thank the many contributors essential to the book's final form: Dena Saxer, for writing a portion of this book, especially the basic step-by-step instructions, and for choosing the title; the artist, Juan Li, for spending many hours drawing and making illustrations of the body's internal functions; Gunther Weil, Rylin Malone, and many of my students for their feedback; Jo Ann Cutreria, our secretary, for making so many contacts and working endlessly; Daniel Bobek for long hours at the computer; John-Robert Zielinski for helping with the new computer system and for rearranging the files and programs to speed up the new process; Helen Stites for editing the book and entering it into the new computer; Adam Sacks, our computer consultant, who assisted in solving computer problems as they arose during the final stages of production; Valerie Meszaros for refining the text and typesetting the book on the new computer; and Cathy Umphress for design and paste ups. Special thanks are extended to Michael Winn for general editing into a form consistent with the Healing Tao Book; to Felix Morrow for his valuable advice in producing the book; and to David Miller for design and overseeing production.

Without my wife, Maneewan, and my son, Max, the book would have been academic—for their gifts, my gratitude and love.

About
Master Mantak Chia

Master Mantak Chia is the creator of the system known as The Healing Tao and is the Founder and Director of The Healing Tao Center in New York. Since childhood he has been studying the Tao way of life as well as other disciplines. The result of Master Chia's thorough knowledge of Taoism, enhanced by his knowledge of various other systems, is his development of The Healing Tao system, which is now being taught in many cities in the United States, Canada and Europe.

Master Chia was born in Thailand in 1944, and when he was six years old he learned to "sit and still the mind" (i.e., meditation) from Buddhist monks. While he was a grammar school student, he first learned traditional Thai boxing and then was taught Tai Chi Chuan by Master Lu, who soon introduced him to Aikido, Yoga and more Tai Chi.

Later, when he was a student in Hong Kong excelling in track and field events, a senior classmate, Cheng Sue-Sue, presented him to his first esoteric teacher, Master Yi Eng, and he began his studies of the Taoist way of life. He learned how to pass life force power from his hands, how to circulate energy through the Microcosmic Orbit, how to open the Six Special Channels, Fusion of the Five Elements, Enlighten-

9

ment of the Kan and Li, Sealing of the Five Sense Organs, Congress of Heaven and Earth, and Reunion of Man and Heaven.

In his early twenties, Master Chia studied with Master Meugi in Singapore, who taught him Kundalini Yoga and the Buddhist Palm, and he was soon able to get rid of blockages of the flow of life force energy in his own body as well as in the patients of his Master.

In his later twenties, he studied with Master Pan Yu, whose system combined Taoist, Buddhist and Zen teachings, and with Master Cheng Yao-Lun, whose system combined Thai boxing and Kung Fu. From Master Pan Yu he learned about the exchange of the Yin and Yang power between men and women and also the "steel body", a technique that keeps the body from decaying. Master Cheng Yao-Lun taught him the secret Shao-Lin Method of Internal Power and the even more secret Iron Shirt method called Cleansing the Marrow and Renewal of the Tendons.

Then, to better understand the mechanisms behind the healing energy, Master Chia studied Western medical science and anatomy for two years. While pursuing his studies, he managed the Gestetner Company, a manufacturer of office equipment, and became well acquainted with the technology of offset printing and copying machines.

Using his knowledge of the complete system of Taoism as the foundation, and building onto that with what he learned from his other studies, he developed The Healing Tao system and began teaching it to others, then trained teachers to assist him, and later established The Natural Healing Center in Thailand. Five years later he decided to move to New York to introduce his system to the West, and in 1979 he opened The Healing Tao Center there. Since then, centers have been established in many other cities, including Boston, Philadelphia, Denver, Seattle, San Francisco, Los Angeles, San Diego, Tucson, Toronto, London and Bonn, among others.

Master Chia leads a peaceful life with his wife Maneewan, who teaches Taoist Five Element Nutrition at the New York Center, and their young son. He is a warm, friendly, and helpful man, who views himself primarily as a teacher. He uses a word processor when writing his books and is equally at ease with the latest computer technology as he is with esoteric philosophies.

He currently is writing an encyclopedia of Taoist Yoga and has published two books: in 1983, *Awaken Healing Energy Through The Tao*; and in 1984, *Taoist Secrets Of Love: Cultivating Male Sexual Energy*. This book is his third volume.

A WORD OF CAUTION

The book does not give any diagnoses or suggestions for medication. It does provide a means to increase your strength and good health in order to overcome imbalances in your system. If there is illness, a medical doctor should be consulted.

1

What Is
The Healing
Tao?

I. The System

The Healing Tao is a self-help system for curing and preventing illness and stress, and for enhancing all aspects of life. Its key concept is increasing vital energy, or Chi, through easy techniques and physical exercises. This life force energy is then circulated through the acupuncture meridians of the body and channeled into health, vitality, balanced emotions, and creative and spiritual expression.

A practical system accessible to everybody, The Healing Tao is a modern expression of centuries-old Taoist practices. Many of these techniques were formerly known only to an elite group of Taoist Masters and hand-picked students. I have formulated these powerful practices into a comprehensive system which I began teaching to the public at large in my native Thailand in 1973. In 1978 I brought this system to the Western world. I then opened The Healing Tao Center in New York and began teaching the practices there. Today we teach our system in various places throughout the United States and Europe. Though spiritual in its foundation, The Healing Tao is not a religion. It is compatible with all religions, as well as with agnosticism and atheism. There are no rituals to perform and no gurus to surrender to. The Master and the Teacher are highly respected, but are not deified.

This book covers the beginning practices of Level 1 of the system:

1. The Inner Smile and
2. Six Healing Sounds.

The entire system has three levels:

1. Level I concentrates on healing energy, strengthening and calming the body;
2. Level II concentrates on changing negative emotions into strong, positive energy; and
3. Level III concentrates on creative and spiritual practices.

All levels include both mental (meditative) practices and physical disciplines, such as Tai Chi, Pakua, and Iron Shirt Chi Kung. The foundation course called the Microcosmic Orbit is covered in my first book, *Awaken Healing Energy Through The Tao*, but is also surveyed in this book as part of a Daily Practice. For a description of other courses and for the addresses and phone numbers of The Healing Tao centers, see the end of this book.

II. Taoism and Some Basic Concepts in Chinese Healing

Taoism is the 5000-8000 year old foundation of Chinese philosophy and medicine. It is also the mother of Acupuncture and the inspiration for modern body-oriented therapies, such as Acupressure, Rolfing and Feldenkrais. The Tao has been described as "natural law" or "natural order", "the constantly changing cycle of the seasons", "an art", "a method", "a power", and "a path of direction".

In the Taoist view, harmony and balance are essential for health. The body is seen as a whole; therefore, stress or injury to one organ, gland or system weakens the entire body. The body is also self-regulating and will naturally move toward balance if allowed to.

Illness is caused by a blockage of energy. Too much or too little energy in one part of the body results in disease to that part and stresses the entire body. The Healing Tao teaches us how to correct this imbalance by awakening the Chi, or vital energy, and circulating it to the needed areas.

The Taoist system links each organ to one of the five elements in nature: metal, water, wood, fire, or earth. It also connects them to a season of the year, a color, and a quality in nature (e.g., wet, dry, windy, etc.). This relationship often describes the characteristics of that organ. For example, the heart is linked to summer, fire and red; a healthy heart is associated with excitement and warmth. The season of an organ is the one in which the organ is dominant or working the hardest.

Body, mind, and spirit are totally integrated in the Taoist view. Therefore, Chinese medicine finds that negative emotions, such as anger, fear or cruelty, and excessive amounts of positive emotions, such as too much joy or excitement, can injure the organs and associated organs and cause disease. Both the Inner Smile and the Six Healing Sounds (covered in this book) help to balance the emotions as well as to improve health.

III.   Illness Starts As a Problem With One's Energy Level

World of Stress

A problem may exist for many years before it physically

manifests itself as a disease. It may appear as a blockage or decreasing of the Chi energy level, leading to a Chi imbalance in particular parts or organs of the body. If we become aware of the Chi imbalance when it first occurs, we have a long grace period in which to correct it.

Many people don't regard bad temper or negative emotions as sickness. In Taoism we regard these as the beginning of the imbalance of the Chi energy in the system, just like bad breath or body odor can be the beginning signs of weakness or illness of the liver, kidneys or stomach.

Stubbornness can be caused by an imbalance of the heart energy. Malodorous sweat can be due to a dysfunction of the kidneys, which have lost the filtering function to eliminate excess water contained in the body fluids. Cowardice and fear can be due to an imbalance of the lung or kidney energy. Back pain can be caused by an imbalance of the kidneys and bladder, and many other bad behaviors and physical ailments can be traced to an imbalance of the Chi energy in different parts of the body.

As we live our lives now, our attachment to the material world grows, and we become more and more drawn to material things, like various drugs, entertainment, services and unnatural foods. The more we feel that we need to have this and buy that, the more worry and mixed emotions we feel. We can get rid of all of these feelings by getting rid of our emotional attachment to these materials.

Conserving, increasing and transforming the Chi energy should be the first or primary preventive method practiced. When a person has a heart attack, he might use this method to prevent a second. When a bad kidney or bad back develops, the use of this method prevents it from getting worse. The primary preventive practices are started at the Chi level. In the Taoist system we map out all the organ energy meridians which have a network extending from the organs throughout the body. When blocked or decreased, the organs are the parts which will get less life force and will trap in the bad Chi (i.e., the Chi we know as sick energy in the organs or the meridians.) If we are not in touch with our inner selves, it is very hard to notice much change internally. By knowing how to conserve, transform and increase the Chi, we have more Chi to open the blockage, increase the body's defensive powers and prevent illness. We can live the happy, healthy life we want to live and maintain our health as we age; we can live life not going from one illness to another, but instead have life-long vitality and a will (desire) to live.

21

The Taoist system is geared to help you live a healthy life, free from illness, with vitality to help other fellow human beings. Many of my students had given up coffee, drinks, drugs, and certain kinds of "necessary" entertainment quite easily when they started to work on themselves to satisfy their organs and senses and thereby strengthen them.

I have one student who, at one time, had many factory workers and, therefore, had power over many people. However, he was deeply in debt because he couldn't give up endlessly buying things. Finally, he came to me and talked to me about his problem. I explained to him that stress and emotional energy created blockages due to energy imbalances in his organs. If he could strengthen his organs and senses and increase the circulation in his body, he would see the world from a different angle. After he completed the Microcosmic Orbit Meditation and practiced the Six Healing Sounds, Inner Smile and Tao Rejuvenation, he came to me and said, "Master Chia, I'm going on a long vacation". I asked, "What happened?" He replied that he had sold his factory, paid all of his debts and had a few thousand dollars left. "I want to rest, practice more of what you teach and come back and start all over again", he said. There was a tremendous change in his face.

IV. The Best Investment is Your Own Health

Many people put all their life force into earning money, until their vitalities are depleted and illnesses set in. They have to spend more and more of their money on hospitals, surgery, medicine, and, finally, spend most of their time in bed.

Many people say, "I don't have time to practice. My day is filled with appointments and work, meetings, study and children." If you can improve your mind, body, and spiritual level of energy, your mind will be clearer; you will be more physically fit; your work will usually take less time to accomplish; and your emotions will be calmer.

Many of my students have the same problem: it is hard to find time to practice the Microcosmic Orbit Meditation, Six Healing Sounds, Inner Smile, Tao Rejuvenation, Tai Chi Chi Kung, Iron Shirt and Fusion of the Five Elements. It takes time to learn in the beginning, but after you learn it, it becomes a part of your life. For example, you can do the Inner Smile while waiting in line. We spend a lot of time each day just waiting, and you can turn that time into practice time.

Many of our students study this system for a while and actually sleep less and eat less, so they end up having more time to do the practice. My knowledge and experience tell me that if people can put a 30-60 minute daily investment into their health each day, they will get 1-4 hours back and will be able to achieve more in less time. As a result, they will have more time to do more things.

V. Taoism in the Home

The Taoists do not regard differing characteristics or personal qualities of the husband and wife as the main sources of unhappiness in the family. The natural thing is for opposites to attract each other. The most important thing is to understand each other, look at each other's strong points, and help to overcome each other's weak points.

In order to understand the other person, you have to understand yourself first. The best way to understand yourself is to get in touch with your own organs through the inner system and senses. You can then strengthen the organs in order to transform negative energy and cultivate positive emotions and values.

Negative emotions are the main causes of energy imbalances in the body. The existence of negative energy in one family member will create negative emotions in other family members and disturb the energy balance in the entire family.

VI. Sexual Imbalances Can Be Modified With Practice

Another factor in the breakdown of the family is an imbalance in the sex life of the married couple. Healthy vitality is a major source of sexual energy. The organs and glands are the main sources of sexual energy, and therefore, healthy organs and glands will increase the happiness of a couple's sex life. A stressful life, pollution, and the vast regulations that govern life in our society rob people of their organ and sexual energies. They are left depressed, with their vitality and sexual energy depleted. This leads to psychological and marital problems. These problems can cause muscular weaknesses, such as impotence (inadequate erection) in men and lack of muscle tone in the sexual organs of women. For a couple, the question is how to increase and transform their sexual energies and therefore correct the physiological problems of the sexual organs. In this book we deal directly with strengthening the internal organs and senses.

VII.   The Peacefulness of Chi Energy

The balance of peaceful Chi energy in a person is very important because it can help to balance the Chi of another person who is close. Anything that is overly extreme will cause an imbalance of Chi energy and will destroy peacefulness. There are five types of peace necessary in a family:

> Peace of mind,
> Peace of the heart,
> Peace of the body,
> Peace of the organs, and
> Peace of the senses.

Taoism says that too much noise will hurt the ears and their associated organs, including the kidneys and the bladder, causing fear and disturbing the peace. Too much drinking or eating will hurt the spleen and indirectly hurt the liver, which will result in anger and bad temper and will disturb the peace of the family. Too much looking at television or movies will hurt the eyes, which will hurt the liver and the gall bladder and cause a loss of energy, weakening the vitality of the entire body. Overexercising or overworking will hurt the tendons. Too much worry will hurt the nervous system.

Weakness of the organs or senses and nerves can cause certain types of unpleasant personal characteristics and bad habits which, in the long run, cause problems for the entire family. By understanding the sources of the problems and using the Inner Smile, Six Healing Sounds and the Tao Rejuvenation exercises and meditations together, the Chi energy imbalance and organ weakness can be treated. It is important to understand the problems and to use the Taoist practices to help family members get over them, in order to avoid larger disturbances. By practicing together, the energies of the family members are exchanged and balanced together as a family unit. When one of the family comes down with a sickness due to stress or negative emotional energy, other members of the family can help to balance that energy before further problems develop.

2

The
Inner
Smile

I. Benefits

A. Low Grade Energy vs. High Grade Energy

In Taoism we regard the negative emotions as low grade energy. Many people operate their lives in anger, sadness, depression, fear, worry, and other kinds of negative energy. These types of energy are bound to cause chronic disease and steal our major life force. The Inner Smile is the true smile for all parts of the body, including all the organs, glands, and muscles, as well as the nervous system. It will produce a high grade of energy that can heal and eventually be transformed into an even higher grade of energy. (Figure IS1).

A genuine smile transmits loving energy, which has the power to warm and heal. Just recall a time when you were upset or physically ill and someone, perhaps a stranger, gave you a big smile—suddenly you felt better. Norman Cousins, former editor of *The Saturday Review*, writes in *Anatomy Of An Illness* that he cured himself of a rare connective tissue disease by watching old Marx Brothers movies. One of my students cured herself of cancer of the breast by continually practicing the Inner Smile to the part that was sick.

In ancient China, the Taoist Masters recognized the power of smiling energy. They practiced an Inner Smile to themselves, which moved Chi energy and produced a high grade of Chi, and achieved health, happiness and longevity. Smiling to one's self is like basking in love, and love can repair and rejuvenate.

The Inner Smile directs smiling energy into our organs and glands which are so vital to life. Ironically, although we

Figure IS1

The Inner Smile will help you have more Chi energy and produces a high grade of Chi.

often pay a great deal of attention to our outer appearance, very few of us are aware of what the inner organs and glands look like, where they're located, or what their functions are. Worse yet, we are insensitive to the subtle warnings they send us when we mistreat them with poor diets and unhealthy life styles. We are like a boss who never pays any attention to his employees and is startled when things go wrong. If we're acquainted with our organs and glands, appreciate what they do, and learn to hear their messages, they will reward us with relaxation and vitality.

B. Honey-like Secretion or Poisonous Secretion

The Inner Smile is most effective in counteracting the stresses of life. In our current society, we spend millions of dollars just to find a way to release stress. Often, these remedies provide only partial and temporary relief.

The Inner Smile has a close relationship with the thymus gland and will increase the activity of that gland. In the Taoist system, the thymus gland is the seat of greater enlightenment, the seat of love and the seat of the life force Chi energy. When we are under emotional stress, the thymus gland is the first to be affected. In the book *Your Body Doesn't Lie* by John Diamond, M.D., Dr. Diamond presents a study that shows that the thymus has a role as the master controller that directs the life-giving and healing energies of the body. The theory of cancer formulated by Sir MacFarlane Burner, the Australian Nobel Prize winner, suggests that increasing the thymus gland's activity will result in a greater ability to ward off cancer. One type of cells produced by the thymus is

T-cells. The function of the T-cells is to recognize abnormal cells and to destroy them. Of the billions of cells produced in the body each day, some will be abnormal. If the T-cells are not activated by the thymus hormone, the abnormal cells will continue to proliferate and develop into clinical cancer. Hence,the thymus gland plays a critical role in the prevention of cancer throughout adult life.

In applied Kinesiology, there is a way to test the strength or weakness of the thymus gland in which the Inner Smile will make an important difference. Have your partner try this test: Touch the thymus, located at the point where the second rib joins the breastbone below the throat. First have your partner not smile, but let the facial muscles drop and the corners of the mouth turn down. Have him keep one hand extended out to the side, while you press the hand down. Then, try it with your partner smiling and see the difference. This demonstrates that when you smile, you activate the thymus gland. (Figures IS3 and IS4).

Figure IS3

The expression in this picture
will increase energy.

Figure IS4

The expression in this picture
can affect your level of energy.

Taoist sages say that when you smile, your organs release a honey-like secretion which nourishes the whole body. When you are angry, fearful or under stress, they produce a poisonous secretion which blocks up the energy channels, settling in the organs and causing loss of appetite, indigestion, increased blood pressure, faster heart beat, insomnia and negative emotions. Smiling into your organs also causes them to expand, become softer and moister and, therefore, more efficient. As a result the liver, for example, has more room to store nutrients and detoxify harmful substances.

The practice of the Inner Smile begins in the eyes. They are linked to the autonomic nervous system, which regulates the action of the organs and glands. The eyes are the first to receive emotional signals and cause the organs and glands to accelerate at times of stress or danger (the "fight or flight" reaction) and to slow down when a crisis has passed. Ideally, the eyes maintain a calm and balanced level of response. Therefore, by simply relaxing your eyes, you can relax your whole body and thus free your energy for the activity at hand. (Figure IS5).

C. Learning Through the Inner Smile

When you are stressed, overly emotional or operating your life in anger or fear, your organs become obstructed and your performance levels are lowered. A lot of energy is eaten up, and you become dull, lacking alertness and playfulness. You are hindered in learning or developing new ideas, and if you try to force yourself to learn, the subject matter often will not remain in your mind and you will not be able to integrate

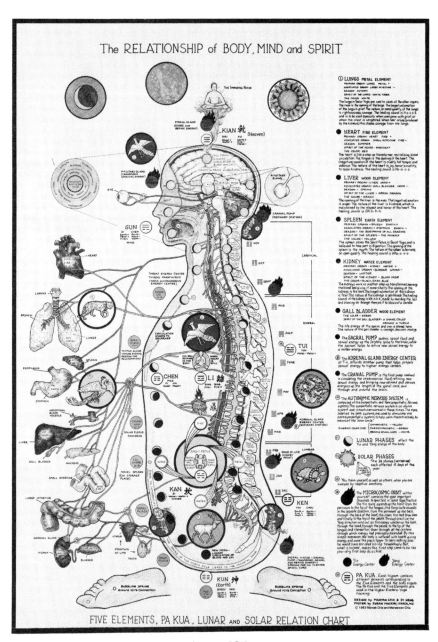

Figure IS5
Eyes linked to autonomic nervous system.

it into yourself. In the Tao system, we believe that our organs, senses and parts of our bodies are involved in learning.

When you smile to your organs, senses and glands, you make a connection and have good communication with them.

When you are stressed or fearful, all the organs and senses are closed. For example, when you do not like someone, your body does not want to accept the person and, thus, is not able to accept that person's teaching and ideas.

1. The main sources of auditory energy

The main sources of auditory energy are the kidney and its associated organ, the bladder. For example, when the kidneys are functioning well, you will be more alert and, thus, able to learn. The kidneys are connected to the openings of the ears. The auditory sense—hearing—is very important in learning. When the kidneys are strong, you will increase your auditory sharpness, which will enhance your learning.

The bladder helps in eliminating toxic fluids, which makes the blood cleaner and the fluids able to flow more freely. If the bladder is impaired, then the kidney functions will be affected.

2. The main sources of the power of speech

The main sources of speech power are the heart and its associated organ, the small intestine. The heart provides the spirit for learning and is the seat of joy. Without eagerness or a spirit to learn, learning will be difficult. The secret of learning is joyfulness, fun and delight. When these are present, your whole body will accept what you learn into itself. The heart is also the seat of respect and honesty. When you have respect, the heart is open. The tongue connects to the heart, and when that connection is open, you can start to accept and program your mind in bits and pieces, assimilating into order what you have learned.

The small intestine helps you assimilate. When the small intestine has a problem, the heart functions are affected. Many times, in order to learn new things, we need time to assimilate them into our systems.

3. The main sources of visual energy

The main sources of visual energy are the liver and its associated organ, the gall bladder. When the liver is in good working order, you will be able to be more assertive, be able to make more decisions, and be able to integrate the things you learn. The opening for the liver is the eyes. When the liver is weak or sick, or you are under stress or are angry, you won't be able to make decisions and your vision will be impaired, making it difficult to program into your mind what you see and to integrate what you learn.

A healthy gall bladder helps you make decisions more easily, too.

4. The main sources of gestational energy

The main sources of gestational energy are the spleen and stomach. The spleen gives the good sense of inclusiveness. It is the opening for the mouth and is involved with the power of speech, the voice, and in digesting what you learn.

The stomach is associated with the spleen. When the stomach is in good condition, you will be more receptive to new thoughts, ideas, and ways. Once you have accepted them as your own, you will be more willing to learn new things and more economic ways.

5. The main sources of olfactory and kinesthetic energies

The main sources of olfactory and kinesthetic energies are the lungs and the large intestine. The lungs are associated with good impulses, and their openings are the nose and skin. They are involved with kinesthetic feeling, the senses of the skin and the sense of touch and feeling, thereby increasing awareness of your surroundings and, so, tremendously increasing your ability to learn.

The large intestine is involved in elimination and release and makes you more open, physically and mentally. When you are constipated, you are more closed, not open to new ideas and not willing to change. Even though only a small step might be required to change, some students will not let go of old ways or ideas to succeed. The large intestine is the associate organ of the lungs and helps strengthen the lungs' functions.

6. The adrenal glands' energy gives you enthusiasm to learn

The adrenal gland gives you vitality and the hot energy, or Yang energy, of the kidney. It also energizes you and makes you enthusiastic to learn. Without vitality you will feel lazy, sleepy and not eager to learn.

7. Thyroid and parathyroid glands help the power of expression

The thyroid and parathyroid glands will help you increase your ability to express your opinions and your experiences so that all the senses can be involved in learning.

8. Thymus gland helps immune system

The thymus gland is the seat of energy, and it helps us in strengthening our immune systems. It creates energy in the form of enthusiasm and, in this way, gives you strength and energy to learn.

9. Sexual organs' energy increases creative power

The sexual organs are the seat of energy for creative power. When you have low sexual energy, you will be less creative and will be stuck in old, inefficient ways. When you know how to smile and increase your sexual energy, you will increase your power to solve problems in daily life.

10. Spine is center of communication

The spine is the center of control and the center of communication. Know how to smile down into your spine and relax it, and you will increase your communication powers; you will know how to communicate what you have learned through your spine into your organs to let them accept new and more efficient ways into your system. The spine is also known as the controller of the networks.

11. The guidelines for super-learning

a. Smile throughout learning. Smile to the parts or organs that are resistant to new ideas. For example, if the heart is unwilling to be accepting and open, smile to it to release the joys and fun of learning. If the liver has too much anger, which shuts off vision, smile to it until it is open.

b. Let your hands, legs, head, chest, eyes, nose, mouth, ears, tongue, anus, etc. all be involved in learning by acting out. For example, if you are learning a new computer, let yourself act or imagine that you are a computer. Get inside and understand it; use your hands, eyes, ears, etc. and let them all be in contact with what you want to learn.

c. Smile to the senses and let them all open and feel light and happy to learn. Let them all be involved in learning. Start from vision; go through the auditory, olfactory, kinesthetic and gustatory senses. Imagine or involve what you are going to learn with your visual sense of what it looks like, with your auditory sense of how it will sound, with your olfactory sense of how it will smell, with your kinesthetic sense of how it will feel, and with your gustatory sense of how it will taste.

d. Use metaphors of your daily life that you know or use the most. For example, if you are a gardener or like flowers, you can connect the thing you know into gardening or flowers. Or if you are an animal lover, transform the things you learn into animals and the characteristics that are like the animals' characteristics.

e. Involve your total self in learning. Check out your whole system—your senses, your organs, your arms, your hands, etc. They are willing to learn and recognize what they don't want to learn. Smile to them; tell them you love them and want them to get involved.

D. Personal Power Through the Inner Smile

1. The smile is the most powerful energy of personal power. The true inner smile from your organs will make all the organs contribute their own power to generate and streamline out to your senses, especially the eyes. The eyes connect to all the organs and senses. Once you know how, you can get power to all the organs.

Imagine we have 63 trillion cells. Each cell gives out a very small millimeter of energy. Multiplied by 63 trillion cells, the energy is tremendous. When you are relaxed and calm and you smile, you can maintain energy at its peak performance and always be ready to take action. The level of energy is always the main clue.

2. When your level of energy increases, you will have more energy to increase your skills, you will have more flexibility of action, and you will know better what you want and how to get it—i.e. specificity.

3. Smile to the sexual organs. The higher the level of sexual energy that you have, the more personal power you will have. When sexual power decreases, personal power decreases, too. Practice how to conserve and increase sexual energy by recycling it. Foods or drugs that claim to increase sexual power are not going to last long, if at all, and can not increase energy or be effective in the long run. Knowing how to cultivate sexual energy is one of the main sources of power.

II. Preparation For The Inner Smile

A. Wait at least an hour after eating to begin the practice.

B. Choose a quiet spot. It might help in the beginning to disconnect the phone. Later on, you will be able to practice almost anywhere with any noise, but for now you need to eliminate distractions in order to develop your inner focus.

C. Dress warmly enough so as not to be chilled. Wear loose fitting clothes and loosen your belt. Remove your glasses and watch.

D. Sit comfortably on your "sitting bones" at the edge of a chair. The genitals should be unsupported because they are an important energy center. This means if you are a man, the scrotal sac hangs free of the edge of the chair. If you are a woman practicing nude, you should cover your genitals with cloth to ensure no energy loss through them.

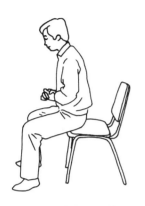  

Incorrect sitting position   Correct sitting position   The back should be straight.

Figure IS8

    E. The legs should be a hips' width apart and the feet should be solidly on the floor.

    F. Sit comfortably erect with your shoulders relaxed and your chin slightly in.

    G. Place your hands comfortably on your lap, the right palm on top of the left. You may find it easier for the back and shoulders to raise the level of your hands by placing a pillow under them. (Figure IS9)

Figure IS9

Close the circuits in the hands, with the left hand on the bottom and the right hand on the top.

H. Breathe normally. Close your eyes. While concentrating, the breath should be soft, long and smooth. After a while you can forget about your breath. Attention to breath will only distract the mind, which must focus on drawing energy to the desired points. There are thousands of esoteric breathing methods; you might spend your whole life mastering them and acquire no lasting energy.

I. Position of the tongue: The tongue is the bridge between the two channels. Its function is to govern and connect the energies of the thymus gland and pituitary gland, and it can balance the left and right brain energies. There are three positions for the tongue. For the beginning, place the tongue where it is most comfortable. If it is uncomfortable to place the tongue on the palate, place it near the teeth. (Figure IS10)

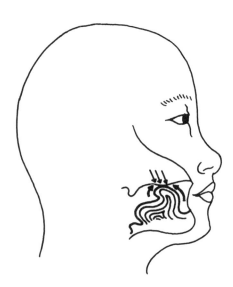

Figure IS10

The tongue

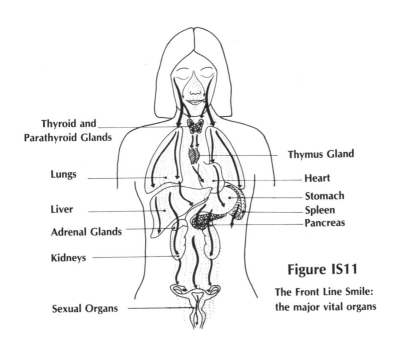

Thyroid and Parathyroid Glands

Lungs

Liver

Adrenal Glands

Kidneys

Sexual Organs

Thymus Gland

Heart

Stomach

Spleen

Pancreas

Figure IS11

The Front Line Smile:
the major vital organs

III. Practice

A. Smiling Down to the Organs
—the Front Line

1. Relax your forehead. You can imagine meeting someone you love or seeing a beautiful sight. Feel that smiling energy in your eyes.

2. Then allow that smiling energy to flow to the midpoint between your eyebrows. Let it flow into the nose, then the cheeks. Feel it relaxing the facial skin, then going deep inside the face muscles; feel it warming your whole face. Let it flow into the mouth, and slightly lift up the corners of the mouth. Let it flow into the tongue. Float the tip of the tongue. Put your tongue up to the roof of the mouth and leave it there for the rest of the practice; this connects the two major channels of energy, the Governor and the Functional. Bring the smiling energy to the jaw. Feel the jaw releasing the tension that is commonly held there.

3. Smile into your neck and throat, also common areas of tension. Although the neck is narrow, it is a major thoroughfare for most of the systems of the body. Air, food, blood, hormones, and signals from the nervous system all travel up and down the neck. (Figure IS12) When we are stressed, the systems are overworked; the neck is jammed with activity, and we get a stiff neck. Be like the Taoist Masters and think of your neck as a turtle's neck—let it sink down into its shell and let it rest from the burden of holding up your heavy head. (Figure IS13) Smile into your neck and feel the energy opening your throat and melting away the tension.

4. Smile into the front part of your neck where the thyroid and parathyroid glands are. This is the seat of your power to speak and, when it is stuck, Chi cannot flow. When it is tense and held back, you cannot express yourself. You will be frightened in front of a crowd, cowardly, and communica-

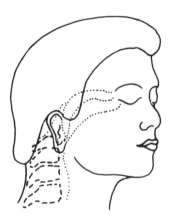

Figure IS12

The neck is a major thoroughfare for most of the body's systems.

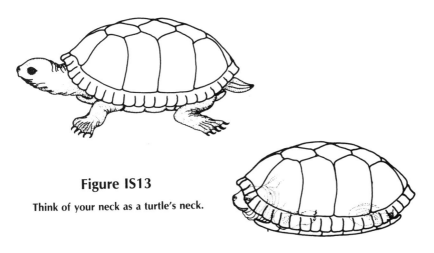

Figure IS13

Think of your neck as a turtle's neck.

tions will break down. Smile dow to the thyroid gland and feel the throat open, like a flower blossom. (Figure IS14)

5. Let the energy of the smile flow down to the thymus gland, the seat of love, the seat of fire, the seat of Chi, and the seat of healing energy. Smile down into it, feel it start to soften and moisten. Feel it grow bigger, like a bulb, and gradually blossom. Feel the fragrance of warm energy and healing Chi flow out and down to the heart. (Figure IS15)

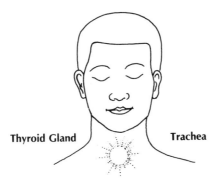

Thyroid Gland   Trachea

Figure IS14

The throat is the seat of your power to speak.

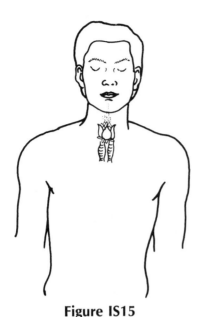

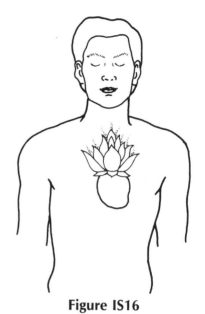

Figure IS15

Feel the thymus gland gradually blossom.

Figure IS16

The heart is the seat of joy;
feel it gradually open like a bulb.

6. Let the smiling energy flow into your heart, which is the size of a fist and is located a little to the left of the center of the chest. The heart is the seat of love, the seat of compassion, the seat of honest respect and the seat of joy. Feel the heart, like a bulb, gradually blossom and send the fragrant warmth of Chi love, joy and compassion radiating throughout all the organs from the pumping of the heart. Let the smile energy fill your heart with joy. Thank your heart for its constant and essential work in pumping blood at the right pressure to circulate throughout you body. Feel it open and relax as it works more easily. (Figure IS16)

7. Bring the smile and joyful energy from the heart to the lungs. Smile into every cell of your lungs. Thank your lungs for their wonderful work in supplying oxygen to the body and releasing carbon dioxide. Feel them soften and become spongier, moister. Feel them tingling with energy.

Smile into the lungs deep inside and smile your sadness

and depression away. Fill the lungs with the fragrance of righteousness that is induced by the love, compassion and joy from the heart. Let the smile energy of joy, love and righteousness flow down to the liver.

8. Smile into your liver, the large organ located mainly on the right side at the bottom of the rib cage. Thank it for its marvelously complex part in digestion—processing, storing and releasing nutrients—and its work in detoxifying harmful substances. Feel it soften and grow moister.

Smile again and get deep into the liver. See any anger and hot temper lying in the liver. Smile them away and let the joyfulness, loveliness, righteousness and warm Chi induce the nature of the liver—kindness—to flow until it is full and overflows out to the kidneys and adrenal glands.

9. Bring the smiling energy into your kidneys, just inside the lower part of your rib cage in the back on either side of the spine. Thank them for their work in filtering the blood, excreting waste products and maintaining water balance. Feel them grow cooler, fresher, and cleaner. Smile into your adrenals, on top of your kidneys; these produce adrenalin for "fight or flight" situations and several other hormones. Your adrenals may thank you by giving you a little extra shot of energy.

Smile again and get deep into the kidneys. See and feel if there is any fear lying inside the kidneys. Smile with the warmth of joy, love, and kindness, and melt your fears away. Let the nature of the kidneys—gentleness—come out and fill them until they overflow to the pancreas and spleen.

10. Smile into your pancreas and spleen. First smile into your pancreas, which is located at the center and to the left at

and above waist level. Thank it for producing insulin to regulate your blood sugar level and enzymes for digestion. Then smile to the spleen, which is at the bottom and left side of the rib cage. Thank it for producing antibodies against certain diseases. Feel it grow softer and fuller.

Smile again into the spleen and pancreas; feel and see deep inside if there is any worry hidden; let the warmth of joy, love, righteousness, kindness, and gentleness melt your worries away. Smile into the virtue of the spleen—fairness—bring it out and let it grow downward to the bladder and sexual region.

11. Bring the smiling energy down to the genital area in the lower abdomen. For women this is called the "ovarian palace" and is located about three inches below the navel midway between the ovaries. Smile into the ovaries, the uterus and the vagina.

For men this is called the "sperm palace" and is located one and a half inches above the base of the penis in the area of the prostate gland and seminal vesicles. Smile down to the prostate gland and the testicles. Thank them for making hormones and giving you sexual energy.

Let love, joy, kindness and gentleness flow into the genital organs so you can have power to overcome and eliminate uncontrollable sexual desires. You are the one who controls your sex drive; it does not control you. Thank your genitals for their work in making you the sex that you are. Sexual energy is the basic energy of life.

12. Return to your eyes again. Quickly smile down into all the organs in the Front Line, checking each one for any remaining tension. Smile into the tension until it is released.

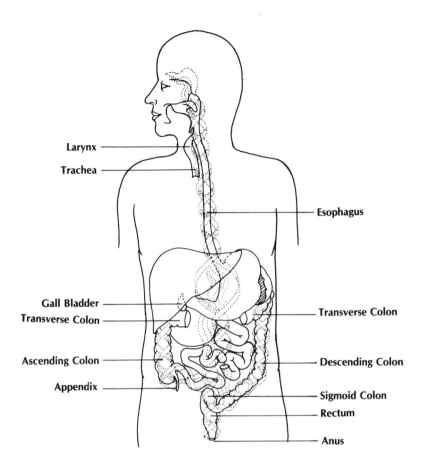

Larynx

Trachea

Esophagus

Gall Bladder

Transverse Colon

Transverse Colon

Ascending Colon

Descending Colon

Appendix

Sigmoid Colon

Rectum

Anus

Figure IS17

Smile down to the digestive system.

B. Smiling Down the Digestive System—the Middle Line

1. Become aware once more of the smiling energy in
your eyes. Let it flow down to your mouth. Become aware of
your tongue, and make some saliva by working your mouth
and swishing your tongue around. Put the tip of your tongue
to the roof of the mouth, tighten the neck muscles, and
swallow the saliva hard and quickly, making a gulping sound

as you do. With your Inner Smile, follow the saliva down the esophagus to the stomach, located at the bottom and below the left side of the rib cage. Thank it for its important work in liquefying and digesting your food. Feel it grow calm and comfortable. Sometimes we abuse our stomachs with improper food. Make a promise to your stomach that you will give it good food to digest.

2. Smile into the small intestine: the duodenum, the jejunum, and the ileum, in the middle of the abdomen. It is about seven meters long in an adult. Thank it for absorbing food nutrients to keep you vital and healthy.

3. Smile into the large intestine: the ascending colon, starting at the right side of the hipbone and passing upward to the undersurface of the right lobe of the liver; the transverse colon, which passes downward from the right liver region across the abdomen to the left beneath the lower end of the spleen; the descending colon, which passes downward through the left side of the lumbar region; and the sigmoid colon, which normally lies within the pelvis, the rectum and the anus. The large intestine is about 1.5 meters long. Thank it for eliminating wastes and for making you feel clean, fresh and open. Smile to it and feel it be warm, nice, clean, comfortable and calm.

4. Return to your eyes. Quickly smile down the Middle Line, checking for tension. Smile into the tension until it melts away.

C. Smiling Down the Spine—the Back Line (Figure IS21)

1. Bring your attention back to your eyes again.

2. Smile inward with both eyes; collect the power of the smile in the third eye (mid-eyebrow). With your inner eyesight direct your smile about three to four inches inside into the pituitary gland, and feel the gland blossom. Direct the smile with the eyes into the third ventricle (third room, the power room of the nervous system, highly magnified). Feel the room expand and grow with bright, golden light, shining throughout the brain. Smile into the thalamus, from where the truth and power of the smile will generate. Smile into the pineal gland and feel this tiny gland gradually swell and grow like a bulb. Move your smile's eyesight, like a bright, shining light, up to the left side of the brain. Move the inner smiling eyesight back and forth in the left brain and across to the right brain and cerebellum. This will balance the left and right brain and strengthen the nerves. (Figures IS18, IS19, and IS20)

3. Move the inner smiling eyesight down to the midbrain. Feel it expand and soften and go down to the pons and oblongata (see illustrations)and to the spinal cord, starting from the cervical vetebra at the base of the skull. Move the inner smiling eyesight, bringing this loving energy down inside each vertebra and the disc below it. Count out each vertebra and disc as you smile down them: seven cervical (neck) vertebrae, twelve thoracic (chest), five lumbar (lower back), the triangular bone called the sacrum, and the coccyx (tail bone). Feel your spinal cord and the back becoming loose and comfortable. Feel the discs softening. Feel your spine expanding and elongating, making you taller.

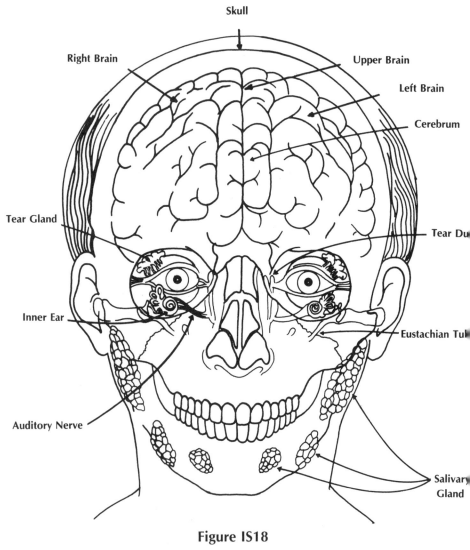

Figure IS18

Parts of the brain

Labels: Skull, Right Brain, Upper Brain, Left Brain, Cerebrum, Tear Gland, Tear Du[c]t, Inner Ear, Eustachian Tu[be], Auditory Nerve, Salivary Gland

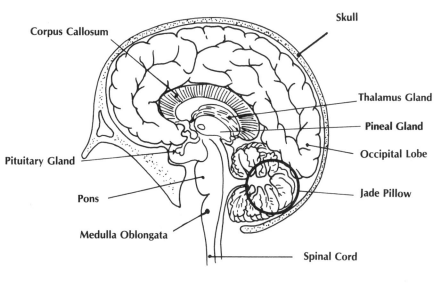

Figure IS19

Side view of mid-brain cross section

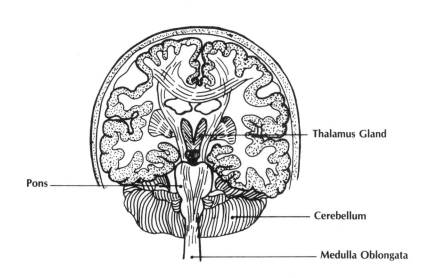

Figure IS20

Frontal view of mid-brain, cross section.

53

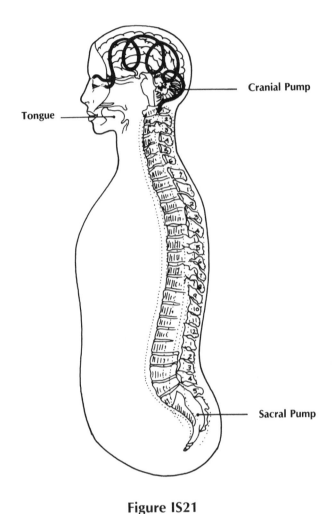

Tongue

Cranial Pump

Sacral Pump

Figure IS21

Bring the loving energy down inside each vertebrae and the disc below it.

4. Return to your eyes and quickly smile down the entire Back Line. Your whole body should feel relaxed. The Back Line exercise increases the flow of the spinal fluid and sedates the nervous system. Smiling into a disc keeps it from

hardening and becoming deformed so it cannot properly absorb the force and weight of the body. Back pain can be prevented or relieved by smiling into the spine.

D. Smiling Down the Entire Length of Your Body

Start at the eyes again. Direct your Inner Smile's eyesight. Quickly smile down the Front Line. Follow the smiling down the Middle Line and then the Back Line. When you are more experienced, smile down all three lines simultaneously, being aware of the organs and the spine.

Now, feel the energy descend down the entire length of your body, like a waterfall—a waterfall of smiles, joy and love. Feel your whole body being loved and appreciated. How marvelous it is!

E. Collecting the Smiling Energy at the Navel

1. It's very important to end by storing the smiling energy in the navel. Most ill effects of meditation are caused by excess energy in the head or heart. The navel area can safely handle the increased energy generated by the Inner Smile. (Figures IS22 and IS23)

2. To collect the smile's energy, concentrate in your navel area, which is about one and a half inches inside your body. Then, mentally move that energy in an outward spiral around your navel 36 times; don't go above the diaphragm or below the pubic bone. Women, start the spiral counterclockwise. Men, start the spiral clockwise. Next, reverse the direc-

tion of the spiral and bring it back into the navel, circling it 24 times. Use your finger as a guide the first few times. The energy is now safely stored in your navel, available to you whenever you need it and for whatever part of your body needs it. You have now completed the Inner Smile.

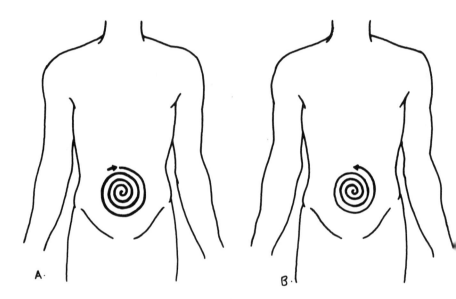

Figure IS22

Collecting smiling energy at the navel for men

A. Collect the energy in the navel, circling it 36 times clockwise and

B. 24 times counter-clockwise.

F. Daily Use

Try to practice the Inner Smile every day as soon as you wake up. It will improve your whole day. If you love your own

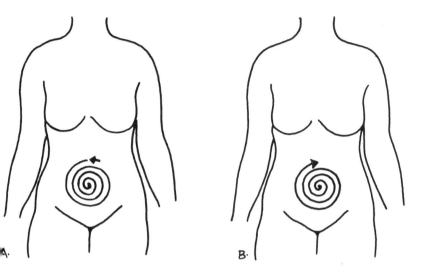

Figure IS23

Collecting smiling energy in the navel for women

A. Collect the energy in the navel, circling it 36 times counter-clockwise, and

B. 24 times clockwise.

body, you will be more loving to others and more effective in your work. Once you have learned it and practiced it regularly you can, if you are short of time, do it more rapidly, in a few minutes.

G. Smile the Negative Emotions Away

Practice it also at times of stress, anger, fear, or depression. Smile down into the part that feels tension and strain, and gradually see the negative energy transform into positive vital life force energy. These draining, negative emotions will be turned into positive energy and vitality. Smile the emotions away. The smile's energy can change emotional energy into vital energy—provided you smile enough into the emotions—such as anger, stress, fear, and impatience.

H. Smile Pain and Sickness Away

If you feel pain and uneasiness in any part of your body, or feel sick in any part of the organs, keep on smiling to these parts; spend more time smiling to these parts, talk to them, get feedback from them, until you feel them get softer or more open or their color changes from dark to bright.

3

The Microcosmic Orbit Meditation

I. Circulate Your Chi In The Microcosmic Orbit (Figure MO1)

The Inner Smile, the Six Healing Sounds and Tao Rejuvenation will gradually increase your life force energy by transforming stress into vitality. To use this energy efficiently and safely for further healing and growth, it must be circulated through specific pathways in your body.

It is much easier to cultivate your energy if you first understand the major paths of energy circulation in the body. The nervous system in humans is very complex and is capable of directing energy wherever it is needed. The ancient Taoist Masters discovered there are two energy channels that carry an especially strong current.

One channel is called the "Functional" or "Yin" Channel. It begins at the base of the trunk, midway between a man's testicles or a woman's vagina and the anus at a point called the perineum. It goes up the front of the body past the sex organ, stomach, organs, heart, and throat and ends at the tip of the tongue. The second channel, called the "Governor" or "Yang" channel, starts in the same place but goes up the back of the body. It flows from the perineum upwards into the tailbone and then up through the spine into the brain and back down to the roof of the mouth.

The tongue is like a switch that connects these two currents—when it is touched to the roof of the mouth just behind the front teeth, the energy can flow in a circle up the spine and back down the front. The two channels form a single circuit that the energy loops around. This vital current circulates past the major organs and nervous systems of the body, giving cells the juice they need to grow, heal, and

The Functional Channel
The Governing Channel

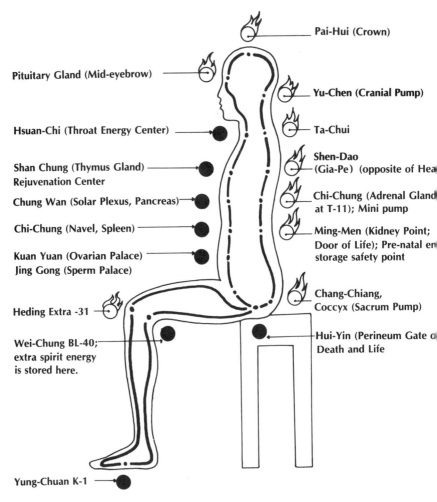

Pai-Hui (Crown)

Pituitary Gland (Mid-eyebrow)

Yu-Chen (Cranial Pump)

Hsuan-Chi (Throat Energy Center)

Ta-Chui

Shan Chung (Thymus Gland)
Rejuvenation Center

Shen-Dao
(Gia-Pe) (opposite of Hea

Chung Wan (Solar Plexus, Pancreas)

Chi-Chung (Adrenal Gland
at T-11); Mini pump

Chi-Chung (Navel, Spleen)

Ming-Men (Kidney Point;
Door of Life); Pre-natal en
storage safety point

Kuan Yuan (Ovarian Palace)
Jing Gong (Sperm Palace)

Heding Extra -31

Chang-Chiang,
Coccyx (Sacrum Pump)

Wei-Chung BL-40;
extra spirit energy
is stored here.

Hui-Yin (Perineum Gate o
Death and Life

Yung-Chuan K-1

Figure MO1

Learn to circulate your Chi in the Microcosmic Orbit to assist in counteracting stress.
The tongue touches the roof of the palate to complete the circuit of the Governing and
Functional Channels.

function. This circulating energy, known as the Microcosmic Orbit, forms the basis of acupuncture. Western medical research has already acknowledged acupuncture as being clinically effective, although scientists admit they can not explain why the system works. The Taoists, on the other hand, have been studying the subtle energy points in the body for thousands of years and have verified in detail the importance of each channel. (Figure MO1)

It is this loop of energy about the body which also carries the organ energy and smiling energy and spreads vitality to other parts of the body.

II. The Importance Of The Microcosmic Orbit

By opening up this microcosmic channel and keeping it clear of physical or mental blockages, it is possible to pump the life force energy up the spine. If this channel is blocked by tension, then learning to circulate the Microcosmic Orbit is an important step to opening up the blockages in the body to circulate and revitalize all parts of the mind and body. Otherwise, when intense pressure builds in the head, much of it escapes out the eyes, ears, nose and mouth and is lost. This is like trying to heat a room while all the windows are open— you're going to have a very high fuel bill.

The way to open the microcosmic energy channel is by sitting in meditation for a few minutes each morning after you do the smile. Allow your energy to complete the loop by letting your mind flow along with it. Start in the eyes, and mentally circulate with the energy as it goes down the front through your tongue, throat, chest and navel and then up the tailbone and spine to the head.

At first it will feel like nothing is happening, but eventually the current will begin to feel warm in some places as it loops around. The key is simply to relax and try to bring your mind directly into the part of the loop being focused on. This is different from visualizing an image inside your head of what that part of the body looks like or is feeling. Do not use your mind as if it were a television picture. Experience the actual Chi flow. Relax and let your mind flow with the Chi in the physical body along a natural circuit to any desired point, e.g. your navel, perineum, etc.

Study of the Microcosmic Orbit is highly recommended to all students who want to better master the transforming of stress and who seek to truly master the techniques taught here. Progress to the higher levels of transforming emotional energy, without first learning the Microcosmic Orbit, is very difficult. Some people may already be "open" in these channels or relaxed when they are close to nature. The benefits of the Microcosmic Orbit extend beyond facilitating the flow of life force energy and include prevention of aging and the healing of many illnesses, ranging from high blood pressure, insomnia and headaches to arthritis.

4

The
Six
Healing
Sounds

I. Benefits And Theory

Thousands of years ago the Taoist Masters discovered in their meditations the six sounds which were the correct frequencies to keep the organs in optimal condition by preventing and alleviating illness. They discovered that a healthy organ vibrates at a particular frequency. To accompany the Six Healing Sounds, six accompanying postures were developed to activate the acupuncture meridians, or energy channels, of the organs. (Figure SS1)

A. Overheating of the Organs

What causes an organ to malfunction? There are many causes. Urban society creates a life full of physical and emotional stresses such as overcrowding, pollution, radiation, junk food, chemical additives, anxiety, loneliness, bad posture, and sudden or overly vigorous exercise. Separately and together, these stresses produce tension and start to block the free passage of energy flow in the body and, thus, the organs overheat. In addition, the concrete jungle that we live in lacks the safety valves provided by nature: trees, open spaces, and running water, which give forth a cooling, purifying energy. Continued overheating causes an organ to contract and harden. This impairs its ability to function and results in illness. One of the surgeons working with The Healing Tao Center in New York reports that the hearts of patients who have died of heart attacks look as if they've been cooked! And the ancient Taoists have a saying: "Stress cooks your brain". (Figures SS2 and SS3)

67

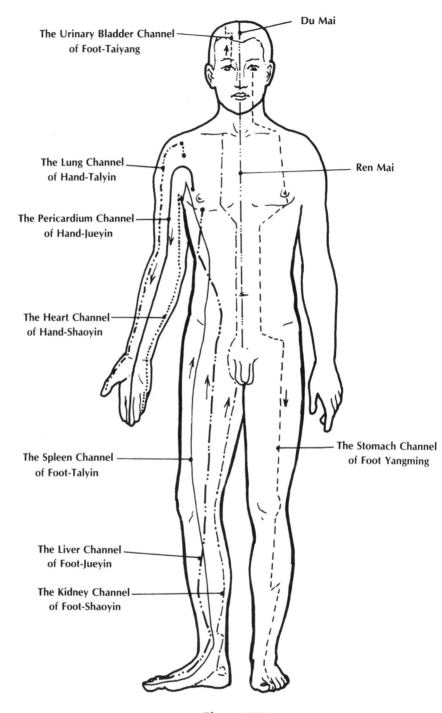

The Urinary Bladder Channel
of Foot-Taiyang

Du Mai

The Lung Channel
of Hand-Talyin

Ren Mai

The Pericardium Channel
of Hand-Jueyin

The Heart Channel
of Hand-Shaoyin

The Stomach Channel
of Foot Yangming

The Spleen Channel
of Foot-Talyin

The Liver Channel
of Foot-Jueyin

The Kidney Channel
of Foot-Shaoyin

Figure SS1

**Distribution of Fourteen Channels
Anterior View**

68

B. The Cooling System of the Organs

Chinese medicine teaches that each organ is surrounded by a sac or membrane, called fascia, which regulates its temperature. Ideally, the membrane releases excess heat out

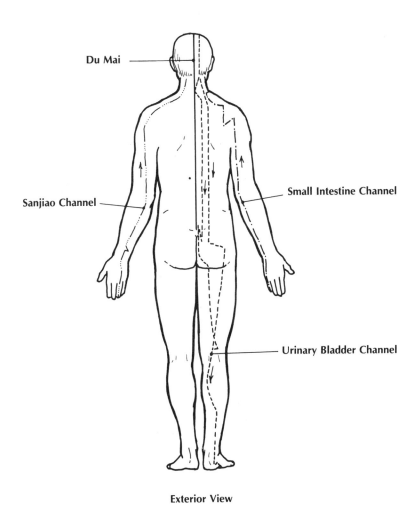

Du Mai

Sanjiao Channel

Small Intestine Channel

Urinary Bladder Channel

Exterior View

69

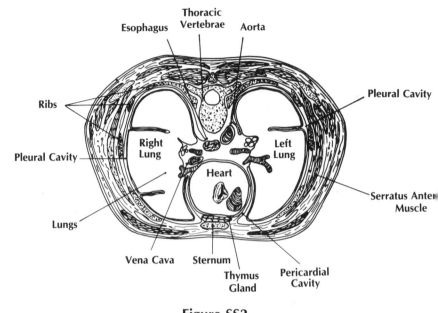

Figure SS2

Cross Section of the thorax

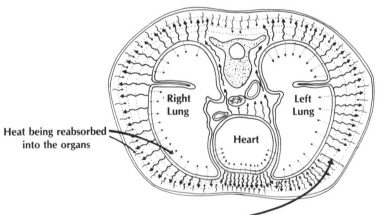

Toxic deposits on tissues and muscles block the free passage
of heat generated by the organs. The heat is reflected back
into the organs, causing pressure, overheating and eventual
malfunction of the organs.

Figure SS3

Over-heating of the organs

through the skin, where it is exchanged for cool life force energy from nature. An overload of physical or emotional tension causes the membrane, or fascia, to stick to the organ so that it cannot properly release heat to the skin nor absorb cool energy from the skin. The skin becomes clogged with toxins and the organ overheats. The Six Healing Sounds speed up the heat exchange through the digestive system and the mouth. The digestive system is more than 20 feet long and runs from the mouth to the anus as one pipe in the middle of the body in between all the organs. It helps release excess heat from the fascia, cooling and cleansing the organs and skin. When all the sounds and postures are done in the proper order, body heat is evenly distributed by the intestinal tract throughout the whole body, and each of the organs is at its correct temperature. (Figure SS4)

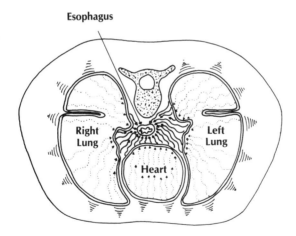

As the sound is made, the heat given off by the organs is transferred out of the body through the esophagus.

Figure SS4

Cooling system of the organs

C. The Sounds That Heal and Prevent

Daily practice of the Six Healing Sounds will restore and maintain calmness and good health. Greater sexual pleasure and improved digestion will occur. Minor ailments, such as colds, flu, and sore throats, can be prevented or thrown off easily. Many students of The Healing Tao have overcome their long-standing dependence on sleeping pills, tranquilizers, aspirin, and antacids. Heart attack victims have prevented further attacks. Several psychologists have taught some of their patients to use the Six Healing Sounds to relieve depression, anxiety or anger; and body work oriented healers have used the Six Healing Sounds to help speed up healing, and the healer spends less of his own life force energy.

Each of the six organs in the practice has an associate organ which responds together with it and in the same manner. When an organ is weak or overheated, its paired organ is similarly affected. Likewise, practicing the appropriate healing sound and posture improves the organ and its associate.

D. The Sensations of the Resting Period

The sensations experienced during the "rest period" of the practice vary from individual to individual. You may feel coolness, tingling, vibration, or lightness or expansion in a particular organ, or your head, hands or legs. Or you may feel nothing specific, just a general feeling of relaxation. You may begin to sense the changes as your organs become softer, moister, spongier and more open.

E. The Best Negative Emotion Control

The Six Healing Sounds are the fastest way to calm down the organs. The "concrete jungle" life that we live tends to trap the pollution and excess heat that surround us in our environment. All kinds of waves stimulate our bodies and organs to hyperactivity. Likewise, the circulation of the life force energy is obstructed, and the energy cannot flow efficiently or easily. When negative energy cannot be expelled from the body, it is circulated and trapped in the organs and in the membrane covering of the organs. The organs themselves begin to overheat, creating more negative emotional energy and added stress.

However, by simply pronouncing the organ sounds, one can release and exchange the gas trapped in the organs. Just as the Taoist Masters of olden times discovered certain sounds that had a close relationship with the organs and which would cool down the organs to their normal temperatures, so can we deliver fresh energy into the organ to release or transform our negative emotions into a more positive or life-giving energy.

F. Getting Rid of Bad Breath

Mouth odor is a most common problem. Many people are not aware of how greatly it affects them personally. People who come in contact with someone with bad breath feel uncomfortable and unpleasant. When you know your breath is bad and you cannot get rid of the persistent odor, you gradually lose confidence in yourself in social gatherings. One of the reasons for bad breath is tooth decay, which can be corrected by a dentist. The other major cause of bad breath is disease of the internal organs. The internal organs, when not healthy, will cause bad breath. A sickly liver, for example, will cause bad breath which smells like decaying meat. The kidneys, when not in a healthy state, will cause breath to smell like fermented urine. A weak or sickly stomach is the main cause of bad breath. When the stomach and the intestines reduce their healthy digestive activities, a great accumulation of partially undigested food remains in their walls, leading to bad breath. The Six Healing Sounds help to detoxify the body, strengthen the organs and release the trapped gases which cause bad breath.

G. Help Get Rid of Body Odor

Strong body odors also make people disliked, especially in the summer. Body odor can be caused by long term work under stress, which makes the organs more nervous and can cause organ pain, especially stomach pain. Stomach pain obstructs the digestive system and the Chi circulatory system. The odor that is secreted when perspiring, especially the odor secreted by the arm pits (which tap the body's energy flow), becomes very strong. The Six Healing Sounds, especially the Lung Sound, can help to exchange the energy and make energy circulate. To do the Lung Sound you have to raise the hands above the head and expose the arm pits. This will help to increase circulating and exchanging the energy in the arm pits so that the organs are more open and cleaner.

The Kidney Sound will also help eliminate bad perspiration. People who perspire easily with little movement or when nervous do so because they have weak kidneys. Their kidneys cannot filter the uric acid out of the body and into the blood stream. When the kidneys are weakened or sick, this filtering system breaks down and an excess build-up of uric acid occurs in the kidneys and throughout the body. This causes a foul smell in an individual's perspiration. When the excess water in the body cannot escape via the kidneys, the body becomes stressed and fear occurs easily, reflecting in foul smelling perspiration. Uttering the Kidney Sound and massaging the kidney area in the back by lightly tapping the kidneys can help to shake the stuck uric acid particles loose from the kidney filters. Massaging the feet at the kidney point, especially at the bubbling spring point on the soles of the feet, will also help greatly.

H. Yawning, Burping and Passing Gas

Yawning, burping or passing gas are common reactions during or shortly after doing the Six Healing Sounds. These aren't socially approved responses in North America, but they are actually beneficial. They're part of the process of releasing trapped bad breath, gas and hot energy from the digestive system. As you inhale, you take cool fresh life force energy into the esophagus and breathe into the organs. Exhaling and pronouncing the correct sound creates an exchange of energy, bringing the good energy to the organ and forcing out the waste energy. The world now spends billions of dollars on antacids and soft drinks to release trapped gas. The Six Healing Sounds do the same thing more efficiently and without expense.

I. Your Best Detoxification is Through Your Own Life Force Energy

Detoxification through the Six Healing Sounds is by far one of the best ways to clean out the organs, because it employs fresh energy to clean them. People spend a lot of money for herbs and drugs in order to cleanse and detoxify the organs. A lot of times substances will enter and remain there, causing more toxicity. Some people will experience moving of gas, or loose or very bad smelling bowel movements; these also are indications of ongoing detoxification.

J. Tears and Saliva

Similar to yawning and burping, practice of the Six Healing Sounds may develop another sign of detoxification: tearing. Tearing helps prevent eye disease and cleanses the organs. Usually cleaning out will also be followed by a spring of saliva from the salivary glands of the mouth, which you will feel to be fresh and fragrant. When you have a lot of saliva, swallow down by pressing your tongue to the roof of your mouth, locking your neck and swallowing.

K. The Sounds Can Increase the Range of Movement

Trapped bad energy in the organs can make the organs tense and painful to contract, thus slowing down many physical activities. However, the Six Healing Sounds release the trapped energy in the organs. In a study by Dr. G. Goodheart, the originator of a practice called Applied Kinesiology, he discovered that each large muscle was related to a body organ. A weakness in a muscle usually meant there was a problem in the Chi energy level of a corresponding organ. In the Taoist system, all organs are associated with movement and the extremities. If there is an obstruction of energy in an organ, trapped bad energy or negative emotions, movement of the muscles paired with that organ will be tense, painful and limited. The muscles are like the back-up tank of the organs. So the range of movement throughout the body will be greatly obstructed and limited when the organs are obstructed with tension or under stress. We find that many of our students improve their range of movement when the tensions are released from within their internal organs after practicing the Six Healing Sounds.

The chart below shows the details of the organs, muscles and emotions associated with them. (Figure SS5).

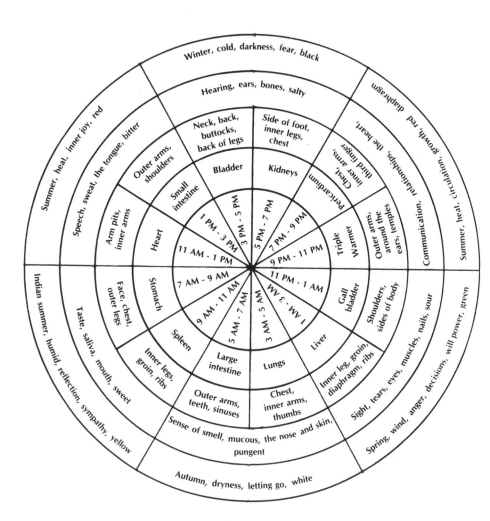

Figure SS5

The Body Clock Chart

II. Preparation For the Six Healing Sounds

A. For maximum benefit, be precise in assuming the position and making the sound for each organ.

B. During all of the exhalation positions, you will be looking up at the ceiling with your head tilted back. This creates a straight path from the open mouth, through the esophagus, down to the organs, and permits a more efficient exchange of energy.

C. The sounds are done sub-vocally—that is, the lips, teeth and tongue produce the sound, but it is heard only internally; this intensifies its power. All sounds are made slowly and evenly.

D. Be sure to follow the order of the exercises as given. This enhances the even distribution of heat in the body. The order follows the natural order of the seasons, from autumn through Indian summer.

E. Wait at least an hour after eating to begin the practice. However, if you have gas, nausea or stomach cramps, you may do just the Spleen Sound right after eating.

F. Choose a quiet spot and take the phone off the hook. Until you've developed a strong inner focus, you need to eliminate distractions.

G. Dress warmly enough not to be chilled. Wear loose-fitting clothes and loosen your belt. Remove your glasses and watch.

III. Position and Practice

A. Sit on your sitting bones at the edge of a chair. The genitals should be unsupported; they're an important energy center. (Figure SS6)

B. The legs should be a hip's width apart, and the feet should be solidly on the floor.

C. The back is straight, shoulders relaxed; sink the chest.

D. Keep the eyes open.

E. Rest the hands on the thighs, palms up. You are now ready to begin the exercises.

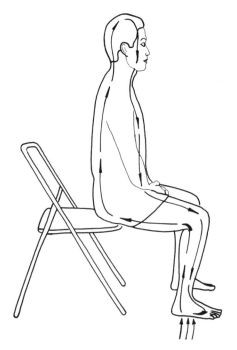

Figure SS6

Sit on your sitting bones at the edge of a chair.

IV. Lung Exercise: the First Healing Sound

A. Characteristics

Lung

Associated organ: large intestine

Element: metal

Season: autumn - dryness

Negative emotions: sadness, grief, sorrow

Positive emotions: righteousness, surrender,

letting go, emptiness, courage

Sound: SSSSSSS

Parts of the body: chest, inner arms, thumbs

Senses: nose - smell, mucous, skin

Taste: pungent

Color: white

The lungs are dominant in autumn. Their element is metal and their associated color is white. The negative emotions are grief and sadness. The positive emotions are courage and righteousness.

B. Position and Practice

1. Become aware of your lungs. (Figure SS7)

2. Take a deep breath and, letting your eyes follow, raise the arms up in front of you. When the hands are at eye level, begin to rotate the palms and bring them up above the head. Keep the elbows rounded. You should feel a stretch that extends from the heels of the palms, along the forearms, over the elbows, along the upper arms and into the shoulders. The

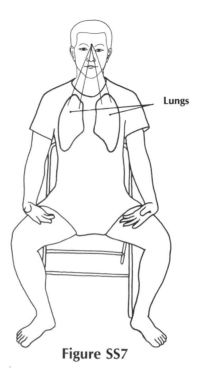

Figure SS7

Become aware of your lungs.

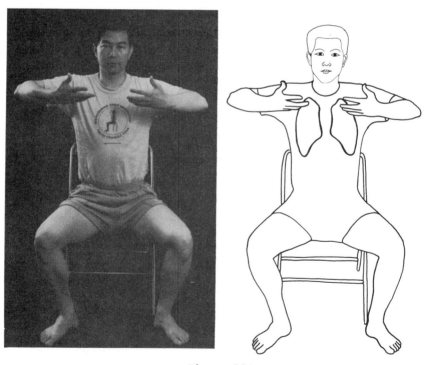

Figure SS8

Rotate your palms and . . .

82

lungs and chest will feel open and breathing will be easier. (Figures SS8 and SS9)

3. Close the jaws so that the teeth meet gently, and part the lips slightly. Draw the corners of the mouth back, exhale, and allow your breath to escape through the spaces between the teeth, making the sound "SSSSSSSS", sub-vocally, slowly, and evenly in one breath. (Figure SS10)

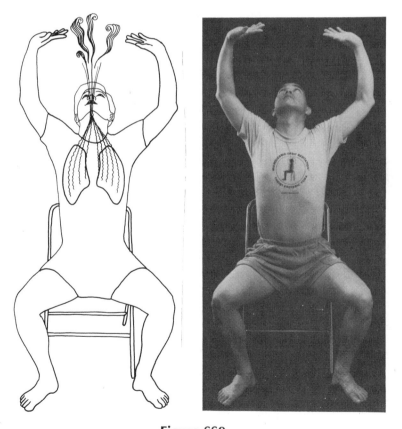

Figure SS9
. . . bring them up above your head.

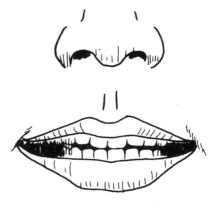

Figure SS10

Mouth Position for Lung Sound
Close the jaws so that the teeth meet. Draw the corners of the mouth back.

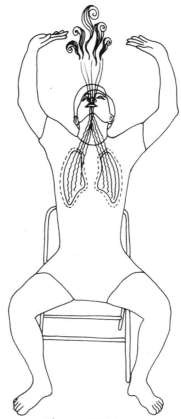

Figure SS11

Picture and feel the sac being fully compressed.

4. As you do this, picture and feel the pleura (the sac that covers the lungs) as being fully compressed, ejecting the "excess heat", sick energy, sadness, sorrow and grief. (Figure SS11).

5. When you have exhaled completely (without straining), rotate the palms down, close the eyes, and breathe in to the lungs to strengthen them. If you are color oriented, you can imagine a pure white light and quality of righteousness entering into your whole lungs. Float the arms down by gently lowering the shoulders. Slowly lower them to your lap so that they rest there, palms up. Feel the energy exchange in the hands and palms.

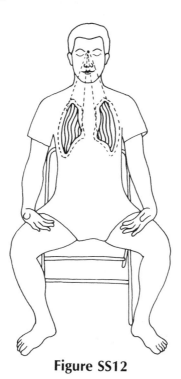

Figure SS12

Close the eyes; breathe normally; smile down to the lungs.

6. Close the eyes, breathe normally, smile down to the lungs, be aware of the lungs, and imagine that you are still making the sound. Pay attention to any sensations you may feel. Try to feel the exchange of cool, fresh energy replacing hot waste energy. (Figure SS12)

7. When your breathing calms down, repeat the sequence 3 to 6 times.

8. For colds, flu, mucous, toothaches, smoking, asthma, emphysema, or depression, or if you want to increase the range of movement of the chest and the inner arm, or for detoxifying the lungs, you can repeat the sound 9, 12, 18, 24, or 36 times.

9. The Lung Sound can help to eliminate nervousness when in front of a crowd. You can do the Lung Sound subvocally without the hand movements several times when you feel nervous in front of a crowd. This will help you to calm down. The Heart Sound and the Inner Smile will help also if the Lung Sound is not enough to calm you down.

V. Kidney Exercise: the Second Healing Sound

A. Characteristics

Kidney

Associated organ: bladder

Element: water

Season: winter

Negative emotion: fear

Positive emotions: gentleness, alertness, stillness

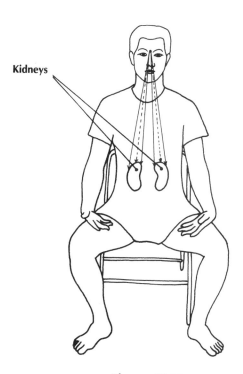

Figure SS13

Become aware of your kidneys.

Sound: WOOOOOOO

Parts of the body: side of foot, inner leg, chest

Senses: hearing, ears, bones

Taste: salty

Color: black or dark blue

Winter is the season of the kidneys. Their element is water and their color is black or dark blue. The negative emotion is fear and the positive emotion is gentleness.

B. Position and Practice

1. Become aware of the kidneys. (Figure SS13).

2. Place the legs together, ankles and knees touching. Take a deep breath as you bend forward, and clasp one hand in the other; hook the hands around the knees; and pull back on the arms. With the arms straight, feel the pull at the back

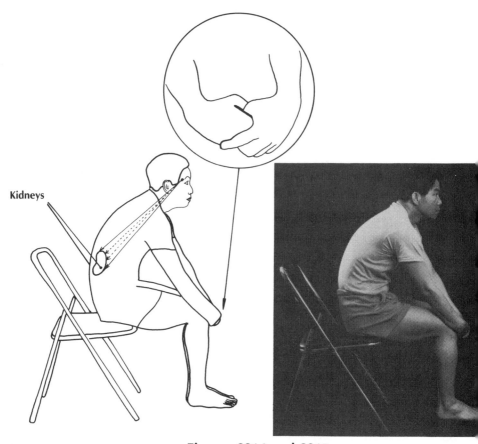

Kidneys

Figures SS14 and SS15

Hook the hands around the knees.

where the kidneys are; look up, and tilt the head back without straining. (Figures SS14 and SS15)

3. Round the lips and silently make the sound one makes in blowing out a candle. At the same time, press the middle abdomen, between the sternum and navel, toward the spine. Imagine the excess heat, the wet, sick energy, and fear being squeezed out from the membrane around the kidneys. (Figures SS16, SS17 and SS18)

4. When you have exhaled completely, sit up and slowly breathe into the kidneys, imagining a bright blue energy as the quality of gentleness enters the kidneys. Separate the legs to a hip's width and rest the hands, palms up, on the thighs.

88

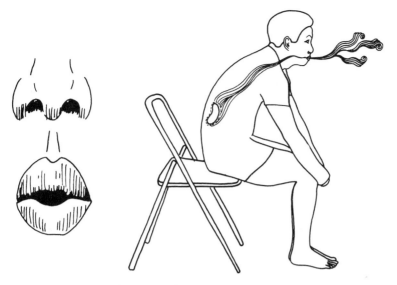

Figures SSI6 and SS17

Round the lips, making the sound one makes when blowing out a candle.

5. Close the eyes and breathe normally. Smile to the kidneys, as you imagine that you are still making the sound. Pay attention to sensations. Be aware of the exchange of energy around the kidneys, and hands, head and legs. (Figure SS19)

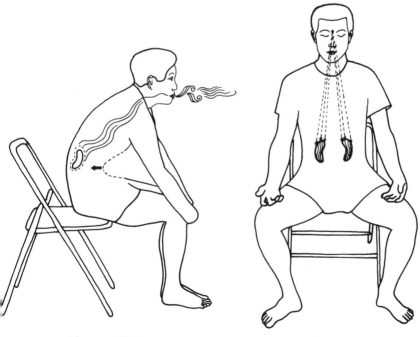

Figure SS18

Press the middle abdomen toward the kidneys.

Figure SS19

Close your eyes and smile down to the kidneys.

6. When your breathing calms down, repeat 3 to 6 times.

7. For back pain, fatigue, dizziness, ringing in the ears, or detoxifying the kidneys, repeat 9 to 36 times.

VI. Liver Exercise: the Third Healing Sound

A. Characteristics

Liver

Associated organ: gall bladder

Element: wood

Season: spring

Negative emotions: anger, aggression

Positive emotions: kindness, self-expansion, identity

Sound: SHHHHHHH

Parts of the body: inner legs, groin, diaphragm, ribs

Senses: sight, tears, eyes

Taste: sour

Color: green

The liver is dominant in spring. Wood is its element and green is its color. The negative emotion is anger. The positive emotion is kindness. The liver is especially important.

B. Position and Practice

1. Become aware of the liver, and feel the connection between the eyes and the liver. (Figure SS20)

2. Place your arms at your sides, palms out. Take a deep breath as you slowly swing the arms up and over the head. Follow with the eyes. (Figure SS21)

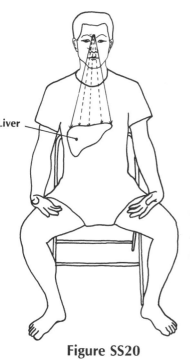

Figure SS20

Become aware of the liver.

Liver

Figure SS21

Slowly swing the arms up and over the head.

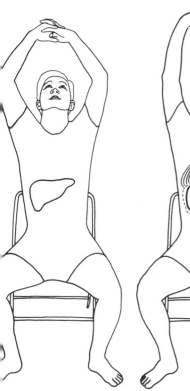

Figure SS22

Interlace the fingers and rotate the palms.

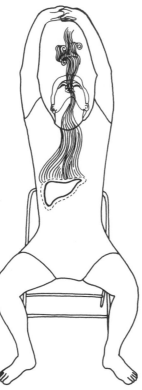

Figure SS23

Push out at the heels of the palms.

Figure SS24

Push more with the right arm.

3. Interlace the fingers and rotate the palms (Figure SS22) to face the ceiling. Push out at the heels of the palms (Figure SS23) and feel the stretch through the arms and into the shoulders. Bend slightly to the left, exerting a gentle pull on the liver. (Figure SS24)

4. Exhale on the sound, "SHHHHHHH" (Figure SS25), sub-vocally. Again, envision and feel that a sac encloses the liver and is compressing and expelling the excess heat and anger. (Figure SS26)

5. When you have exhaled completely, unlock the fingers, and pressing out with the heels of the palms (Figure SS27), breathe into the liver slowly; imagine a bright green color quality of kindness entering the liver. Gently bring the arms back to the side by lowering the shoulders. Place your hands on your lap, palms up, and rest.

6. Close the eyes, breathe normally, smile down to the liver and imagine you're still making the sound. Be aware of sensations. Sense the energy exchange. (Figure SS28)

7. Do this 3 to 6 times. For anger, red and watery eyes, or a sour or bitter taste, and for detoxifying the liver, repeat 9 to 36 times.

A Taoist axiom about controlling anger says: If you've done the Liver Sound 30 times and you are still angry at someone, you have the right to slap that person.

Figure SS25   Exhale on the sound "SHHHHHHH"

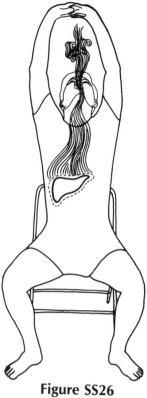

Figure SS26

Feel that a sac encloses the liver and is compressing.

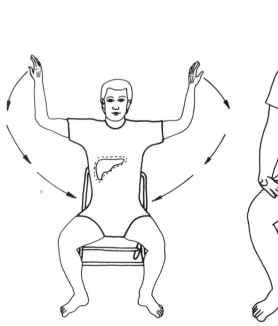

Figure SS27

Press out with the heels of the palms.

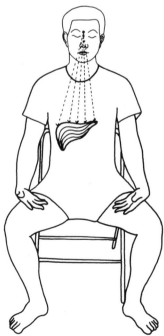

Figure SS28

Close your eyes and smile down to the liver.

VII. Heart Exercise: the Fourth Healing Sound

A. Characteristics

Heart

Associated organ: small intestine

Element: fire

Season: summer

Negative emotions: impatience, arrogance,
hastiness, cruelty, violence

Positive emotions: joy, honor, sincerity,
creativity, enthusiasm, spirit, radiance, light

Sound: HAWWWWWW

Parts of the body: arm pits, inner arms

Senses: tongue, speech

Taste: bitter

Color: red

The heart is constantly working, beating at the rate of approximately 72 times a minute, 4,320 times an hour, 102,680 times each day. This naturally produces heat, which is dissipated by the heart's sac, the pericardium. In the Taoist view, the pericardium is important enough to be considered a separate organ.

B. Position and Practice

1. Become aware of the heart and feel the tongue connected with the heart. (Figure SS29).

2. Take a deep breath and assume the same position as for the Liver Sound (Figure SS30), but lean slightly to the right (Figure SS31).

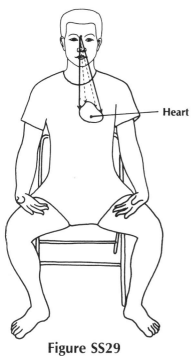

Figure SS29

Become aware of the heart.

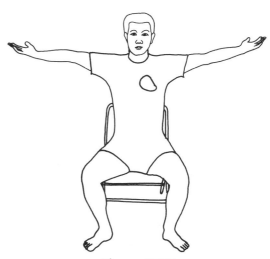

Figure SS30

Assume the same position as for the Liver Sound.

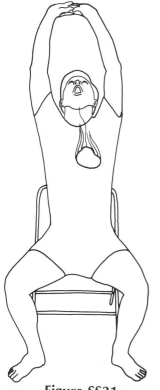

Figure SS31

Push more with the left arm.

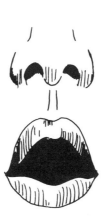

Figure SS32

Open mouth, rounded lips.

95

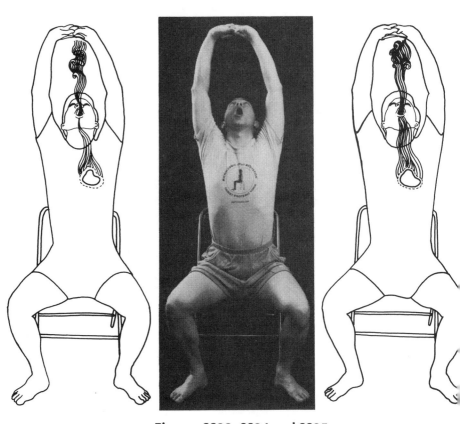

Figures SS33, SS34 and SS35
Open your mouth somewhat, round your lips and exhale on the sound "HAAAAAAW".

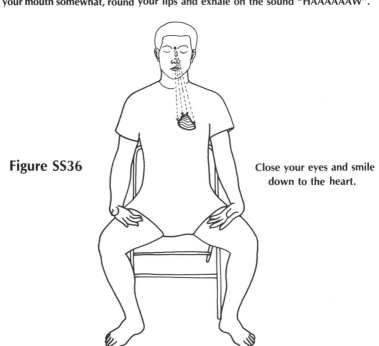

Figure SS36

Close your eyes and smile down to the heart.

3. Open the mouth somewhat (Figure SS32), round the lips and exhale on the sound "HAWWWWWW" (Figures SS33, SS34 and SS35), sub-vocally, as you picture the pericardium releasing heat, impatience, arrogance and hastiness.

4. For the rest cycle, repeat the procedure for the Liver Sound, but focus attention on your heart (Figure SS36) and imagine a bright red color and the qualities of joy, honor, sincerity and creativity entering the heart.

5. Do 3 to 6 times. For a sore throat, cold sores, swollen gums or tongue, heart disease, heart pains, jumpiness, moodiness, and for detoxifying the heart, repeat 9 to 36 times.

VIII. Spleen Exercise: the Fifth Healing Sound

A. Characteristics
Associated organs: pancreas, stomach
Element: earth
Season: Indian summer
Negative emotions: worry, sympathy, pity
Positive emotions: fairness, compassion,
    centering, music making

Sound: WHOOOOOO
Taste: neutral
Color: yellow

B. Position and Practice

1. Become aware of the spleen; feel the mouth and the spleen connect. (Figure SS37)

2. Take a deep breath as you place your hands (Figure SS38) with the index fingers resting at the bottom and slightly to the left of the sternum. (Figure SS39). Press in with the fingers as you push out with the middle back. (Figure SS40).

3. Exhale on the sound "WHOOOOOO" (Figure SS41), made sub-vocally and felt in the vocal chords (Figure SS42). Expel the excess heat, wetness and dampness, and worry, sympathy and pity.

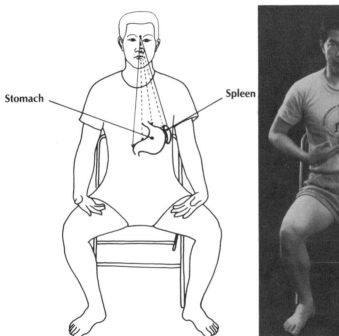

Stomach   Spleen

Figure SS37
Become aware of the spleen.

Figure SS38
Take a deep breath.

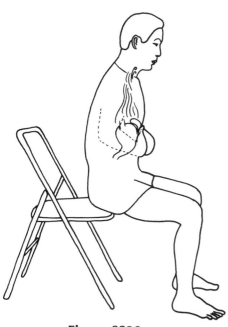

Figure SS39

Place your hands with the index fingers resting at the bottom and slightly to the left of the sternum.

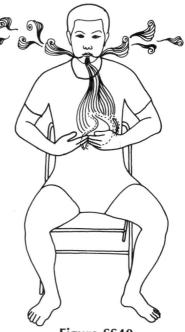

Figure SS40

Press in with the fingers.

Figure SS41

Exhale on the sound "WHOOOOOO".

Figure SS42

Feel the sound in the vocal chords.

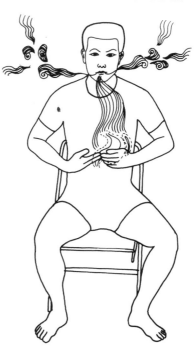

4. Breathe into the spleen, pancreas, and stomach (Figure SS43), or imagine a bright yellow light, and the qualities of fairness, compassion, centering, and music making entering them.

5. Lower the hands slowly to your lap, palms up.

6. Close the eyes, breathe normally and imagine you are still making the sound. Be aware of sensations and the exchange of energy. (Figure SS44)

7. Repeat 3 to 6 times.

8. Repeat 9 to 36 times for indigestion, nausea and diarrhea, and for detoxifying the spleen. This sound, done in conjunction with the others, is more effective and healthier than using antacids. It is the only sound that can be done immediately after eating.

Figure SS43	**Figure SS44**
Breathe into the spleen, pancreas and stomach.	Close your eyes and smile down to the spleen, pancreas and stomach.

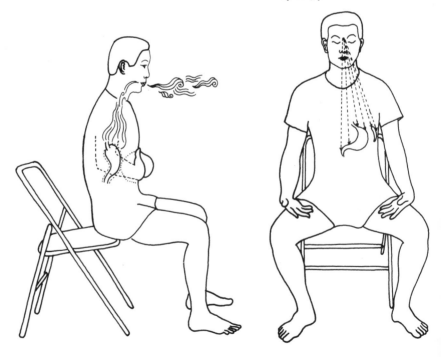

IX. Triple Warmer Exercise (Or Circulation Sex): the Sixth Healing Sound

A. Characteristics

The Triple Warmer refers to the three energy centers of the body. The upper level, which consists of the brain, heart, and lungs, is hot. The middle section, consisting of the liver, kidneys, stomach, pancreas, and spleen, is warm. The lower level containing the large and small intestines, the bladder, and the sexual organs, is cool. The Triple Warmer Sound balances the temperature of the three levels by bringing hot energy down to the lower center and cold energy up to the upper center, through the digestive tract. This induces a deep, relaxing sleep. A number of students have been able to break a long-standing dependence on sleeping pills by practicing this sound. It's also very effective for relieving stress.

There is no season, color, or emotion associated with the Triple Warmer.

B. Position and Practice

1. Lie down on your back. Elevate the knees with a pillow if you feel any pain in the small of the back or lumbar area.

2. Close the eyes and take a deep breath, expanding the stomach and chest without strain. (Figures SS45 and SS46)

3. Exhale on the sound "HEEEEEEE" (Figure SS47), made sub-vocally, as you picture and feel a large roller pressing out your breath, beginning at the top of the chest and ending at the lower abdomen. Imagine the chest and abdo-

men are as flat as a sheet of paper, and feel light, bright, and empty. (Figures SS48, SS49, SS50, SS51 and SS52) Rest by breathing normally. (Figure SS52)

4.   Repeat 3 to 6 times, or more, if you are still wide awake. The Triple Warmer Sound also can be used to relax, without falling asleep, by lying on your side or sitting in a chair. (Figure SS53)

Figure SS45

Lie on your back; close the eyes; take a deep breath.

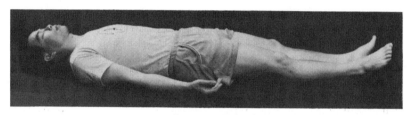

Figure SS46

Organs' diagram.

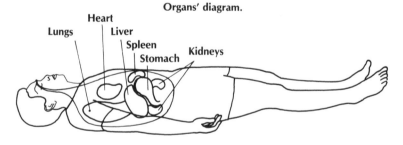

Figure SS47

Figure SS48

Figure SS49

Figure SS50

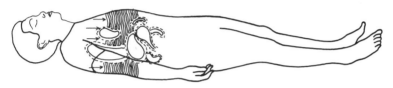

Figure SS51

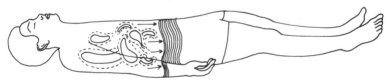

Figure SS52

Rest by breathing normally.

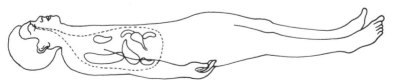

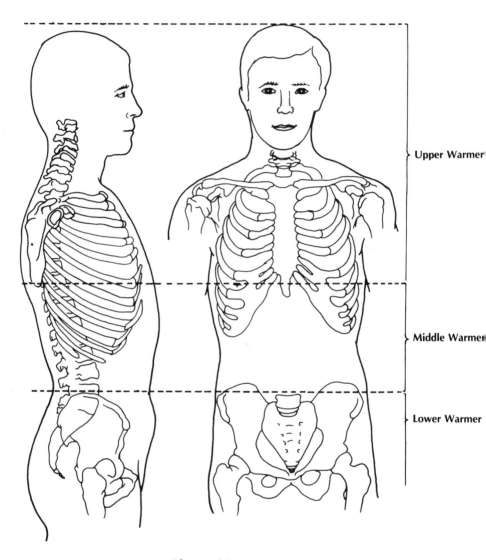

Upper Warmer

Middle Warmer

Lower Warmer

Figure SS53

The Triple Warmer

X. Daily Use

A. Try to Practice the Six Healing Sounds Daily.

Any time of the day is fine. It is especially effective at bedtime because it induces a deep, relaxing sleep. Once you have learned the procedure, it takes only 10-15 minutes.

B. Release the Heat after Vigorous Exercise

Do the Six Healing Sounds right after vigorous exercise, such as aerobics, jogging, martial arts, or after any type of yoga or meditation that creates a lot of heat in the upper warmer (the brain or the heart). This prevents the dangerous over-heating of the organs that can otherwise occur. Do not take a cold shower right after vigorous exercise; it's too much of a shock to the organs.

C. Do the Sounds in Proper Sequence

1. Always do them in the proper sequence: Lung Sound (autumn), Kidney Sound (winter), Liver Sound (spring), Heart Sound (summer), Spleen Sound (Indian summer), Triple Warmer Sound.

2. If a particular organ or its accompanying symptom is bothering you, increase the number of times you do that individual sound without going through the whole sequence.

D. Season, Organ, and Sound

An organ works harder, and thus creates more heat, during the season in which it is dominant. Therefore, increase the number of times you do its exercise. For example, in spring do the Liver Sound 6 to 9 times while doing the other sounds 3 to 6 times.

If you are very pressed for time or very fatigued, only do the lung and kidney exercises.

E.   Get in Touch During the Resting Period

The resting period in between each sound is very important. It is the time that you are becoming in touch with, and more aware of, the organs. Often times when you rest and smile into the organ, you can feel the exchange of the Chi energy in the organ, the hands and the legs. The head also feels the energy flow. Take as much time as you desire during the rest periods.

5

Taoist Daily Life Wisdom

I. Smile Away the Stress

Remember always to smile sincerely with your eyes and to fill your heart with love. This acts as a preventive medicine. When you are sad, angry, crying, depressed or nervous, your organs secrete poisons; but when you are happy and smile, they produce a honey-like, health giving secretion instead.

It is common knowledge that life today is very hectic. Ending the work- day with a headache has become a way of life for many. With pressures building seemingly all around you and within you, "something has to be done." Oddly, the thing to do is not to do anything. When a trying situation arises, no matter what it might be, you have to learn not to be drawn in by it. The way to be able to do that is to smile. In that simple act the world is made over, and what would otherwise have been troublesome never seems to arise.

At first, it may prove to be very difficult to comprehend the results of the Inner Smile, let alone to make it into a new experience; but, with sufficient practice, you can make it an integral part of your life.

Wherever you are—standing, walking, or sitting—remember to smile, and relax, to fill your heart with love and to let the loving feeling spread throughout your whole body. It is so very simple and yet so very effective. Just cultivate a peaceful, loving heart; smile easily and your troubles will melt away.

II. Speak With Thought

Speak less; choose carefully what you say and when and how you say it. Speaking appropriately can be a blessing to all, and speaking less conserves Chi.

III. Worry Less; Take Action More

Think less about the future and the past, because those are the things that worry builds on, and worry produces stress.

Try instead to concentrate whenever you can—remember that concentration happens and is not something that you make happen—and cultivate attitudes of helping and of forgiveness in your daily life.

IV. Cultivating Mental Power

Taoist methods involve the cultivation of generative and mental power. The word for mind also means heart in many oriental languages, just as in Chinese. When you develop to the stage of no longer being concerned with personal ambition, when you are able to forget yourself and cultivate your heart, you have at hand the means of being free from illness.

When you are ill and meditate, do not think that you are doing it escape from your illness. Instead, simply concentrate on a prescribed point or method and everything else will drop away.

V. *Control Your Sex Life; Do Not Let It Control You*

Curb your sexual activity. Too frequent ejaculation will greatly reduce your store of Chi and your ability to concentrate.

The mind is troubled by what is fed to it through the eyes, ears, mouth, nose and mind - i.e., the senses. When we are young and are exposed to sexually stimulating reading matter, we are not equipped to deal properly with it in a way which would conserve our energy. Therefore, it is advised that you concentrate on your daily practice and avoid "distractions".

VI. *Respect Your Head; Warm Your Feet*

Regard your head with the greatest respect. Think of it as a temple of God and of the mind. See it as the temple of the soul and the main control of all the vital organs. There is a rule of thumb to abide by which is "Cool head, warm feet". This will insure you against collecting too much power in your head, thereby possibly causing you discomfort and possibly illness. When power goes to the head, high blood pressure can develop. Directing the power down to the feet can relieve the pressure, and keeping the feet warm can guard you against heart attack. So rub your feet and keep them warm. When you finish, you must always store the energy in the navel and keep it warm.

VII. *Keep Your Neck Warm*

The neck has many important blood vessels and nerves and connects to that very important part of you, the head. So treat it well, too; keep it warm and loose by pervading it with a smile.

Try not to use your senses too much. Don't look at or listen to anything for too long at a time. Whenever the senses are used excessively, sickness can result.

Overindulge yourself with too much food and drink, and you will cause yourself ill health.

To prolong your life and avoid illness, practice swallowing your saliva many times a day.

Do not expose yourself to the wind after bathing or perspiring.

Replace the unpurified Chi of your body with pure original Chi, by practicing the Microcosmic Orbit and by opening all of the 32 routes.

Please the divinities within, and you may in time progress toward immortality.

VIII. *Wisdom in Eating*

Do not overeat until you are too full and then lie down or sit for a long time, as such practice will surely shorten your life.

Eat short of satiation, and then take a leisurely stroll; and do not eat at all at night before retiring.

Eat small amounts of food and eat more frequently. In this way you will be assured of proper digestion and of not over-taxing your five organs.

When eating, eat hot foods first, then warm; and if there is no cold food, drink some cold water. Always, before eating, inhale slightly and swallow some air.

Eat more pungent food in the spring, more sour food in the summer, more bitter food in autumn, and less salty food in winter, but do not be excessive in doing this.

In general, cooked food is better than uncooked, and eating a little is better than eating a lot.

If you have eaten too much, be careful not to drink too much water and not to gulp it down suddenly.

Indigestion follows when you eat to satiation after having been hungry for a long time.

Do not eat raw fruit on an empty stomach, because it heats above the diaphragm.

Too many raw vegetables can upset one's healthy color.

IX. Do Not Do These to Excess

Walking too long harms the tendons; sitting too long harms the flesh; standing too long harms the bones; lying down too long harms vital energy; and gazing too long harms the blood.

Anger, grief, pity and melancholy are harmful, as is too much joy or pleasure. Suffering is harmful; abstinence from sexual activity is harmful; to be anxious is harmful. In short, to neglect moderation is harmful.

X. Joy Increases the Chi

With great joy, the vital Chi soars.

Great sadness causes the flow of Chi to stop.

You can exhaust your vital energy by too frequent sexual activity.

To swallow saliva is to increase its essence. When it is not swallowed it loses strength.

When you are ill, do not lie with your head to the north.

Right after awakening from sleeping, talking too much robs you of vital energy.

XI. Seasonal Health Care

During winter, see to it that your feet are warm and allow your head to be cool. In the spring and autumn permit both your head and feet to be cool.

When ill and perspiring, do not drink cold water as this will damage your heart and stomach.

When lying down in spring and summer have your head face east, whereas in autumn and winter it should face west.

To be free of sickness, a Master squats to urinate before eating and stands to urinate after eating.

When sleeping, bend the knees and lie on your side. This increases your vital energy.

In summer and autumn go to sleep early and arise early;

in winter retire early and arise late; and in spring go to sleep while there is daylight and arise early.

At dawn, midday, during the afternoon, at twilight and at midnight, clean your teeth and rinse your mouth seven times; this will lengthen your life and strengthen your bones, teeth, muscles, nails and hair.

THE
INTERNATIONAL
HEALING TAO SYSTEM

The Goal of the Taoist Practice

The Healing Tao is a practical system of self-development that enables the individual to complete the harmonious evolution of the physical, mental, and spiritual planes the achievement of spiritual independence. Through a series of ancient Chinese meditative and internal energy exercises, the practitioner learns to increase physical energy, release tension, improve health, practice self-defense, and gain the ability to heal oneself and others. In the process of creating a solid foundation of health and well-being in the physical body, the basis for developing one's spiritual independence is also created. While learning to tap the natural energies of the Sun, Moon, Earth, and Stars, a level of awareness is attained in which a solid spiritual body is developed and nurtured.

The ultimate goal of the Tao practice is the transcendence of physical boundaries through the development of the soul and the spirit within man.

International Healing Tao Course Offerings

There are now many International Healing Tao centers in the United States, Canada, West Germany, Switzerland, Austria, Belgium, France, South America, India, and Australia offering personal instruction in various practices including the Microcosmic Orbit, the Healing Love Meditation, Tai Chi Chi Kung, Iron Shirt Chi Kung, and the Fusion Meditations.

Healing Tao Warm Current Meditation, as these practices are also known, awakens, circulates, directs, and preserves the generative life-force called Chi through the major acupuncture meridians of the body. Dedicated practice of this ancient, esoteric system eliminates stress and nervous tension, massages the internal organs, and restores health to damaged tissues.

Outline of the Complete System of The Healing Tao

Courses are taught at our various centers. Direct all written inquiries to one central address or call:

The Healing Tao Center
P.O. Box 1194
Huntington, NY 11743
516-367-2701

INTRODUCTORY LEVEL I: Awaken Your Healing Light

Course 1: (1) Opening of the Microcosmic Channel; (2) The Inner Smile; (3) The Six Healing Sounds; and (4) Tao Rejuvenation—Chi Self-Massage.

INTRODUCTORY LEVEL II: Development of Internal Power

Course 2: Healing Love: Seminal and Ovarian Kung Fu.

Course 3: Iron Shirt Chi Kung; Organs Exercise and Preliminary Rooting Principle. The Iron Shirt practice is divided into three workshops: Iron Shirt I, II, and III.

Course 4: Fusion of the Five Elements, Cleansing and Purifying the Organs, and Opening of the Six Special Channels. The Fusion practice is divided into three workshops: Fusion I, II, and III.

Course 5: Tai Chi Chi Kung; the Foundation of Tai Chi Chuan. The Tai Chi practice is divided into seven workshops: (1) Original Thirteen Movements' Form (five directions, eight movements); (2) Fast Form of Discharging Energy; (3) Long Form (108 movements); (4) Tai Chi Sword; (5) Tai Chi Knife; (6) Tai Chi Short and Long Stick; (7) Self-Defense Applications and Mat Work.

Course 6: Taoist Five Element Nutrition; Taoist Healing Diet.

INTRODUCTORY LEVEL III: The Way of Radiant Health

Course 7: Healing Hands Kung Fu; Awaken the Healing Hand—Five Finger Kung Fu.

Course 8: Chi Nei Tsang; Organ Chi Transformation Massage. This practice is divided into three levels: Chi Nei Tsang I, II, and III.

Course 9: Space Dynamics; The Taoist Art of Energy Placement.

INTERMEDIATE LEVEL: Foundations of Spiritual Practice

Course 10: Lesser Enlightenment Kan and Li: Opening of the Twelve Channels; Raising the Soul, and Developing the Energy Body.

Course 11: Greater Enlightenment Kan and Li: Raising the Spirit and Developing the Spiritual Body.

Course 12: Greatest Enlightenment: Educating the Spirit and the Soul; Space Travel.

ADVANCED LEVEL: The Realm of Soul and Spirit

Course 13: Sealing of the Five Senses.

Course 14: Congress of Heaven and Earth.

Course 15: Reunion of Heaven and Man.

Course Descriptions of The Healing Tao System

INTRODUCTORY LEVEL I: Awaken Your Healing Light

Course 1:
A. The first level of the Healing Tao system involves opening the Microcosmic Orbit within yourself. An open Microcosmic Orbit enables you to expand outward to connect with the Universal, Cosmic Particle, and Earth Forces. Their combined forces are considered by Taoists as the Light of Warm Current Meditation.

Through unique relaxation and concentration techniques, this practice awakens, circulates, directs, and preserves the generative life-force, or Chi, through the first two major acupuncture channels (or meridians) of the body: the Functional Channel which runs down the chest, and the Governor Channel which ascends the middle of the back.

Dedicated practice of this ancient, esoteric method eliminates stress and nervous tension, massages the internal organs, restores health to damaged tissues, increases the consciousness of being alive, and establishes a sense of well-being. Master Chia and certified instructors will assist students in opening the Microcosmic Orbit by passing energy through their hands or eyes into the students' energy channels.

B. *The Inner Smile* is a powerful relaxation technique that utilizes the expanding energy of happiness as a language with which to communicate with the internal organs of the body. By learning to smile inwardly to the organs and glands, the whole body will feel loved and appreciated. Stress and tension will be counteracted, and the flow of Chi increased. One feels the energy descend down the entire length of the body like a waterfall. The Inner Smile will help the student to counteract stress, and help to direct and increase the flow of Chi.

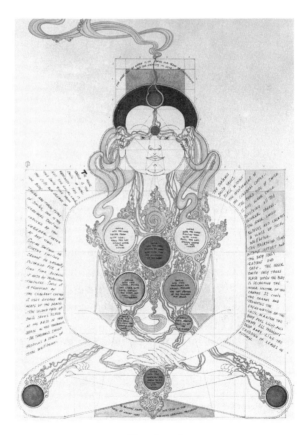

C. *The Six Healing Sounds* is a basic relaxation technique utilizing simple arm movements and special sounds to produce a cooling effect upon the internal organs. These special sounds vibrate specific organs, while the arm movements, combined with posture, guide heat and pressure out of the body. The results are improved digestion, reduced internal stress, reduced insomnia and headaches, and greater vitality as the Chi flow increases through the different organs.

The Six Healing Sounds method is beneficial to anyone practicing various forms of meditation, martial arts, or sports in which there is a tendency to build up excessive heat in the system.

D. *Taoist Rejuvenation—Chi Self-Massage* is a method of hands-on self-healing work using one's internal energy, or Chi, to strengthen and rejuvenate the sense organs (eyes, ears, nose, tongue), teeth, skin, and inner organs. Using internal power (Chi) and gentle external stimulation, this simple, yet highly effective, self-massage technique enables one to dissolve some of the energy blocks and stress points responsible for disease and the aging process. Taoist Rejuvenation dates back 5000 years to the Yellow Emperor's classic text on Taoist internal medicine.

Completion of the Microcosmic Orbit, the Inner Smile, the Six Healing Sounds, and Tao Rejuvenation techniques are prerequisites for any student who intends to study Introductory Level II of the Healing Tao practice.

INTRODUCTORY LEVEL II: Development of Internal Power

Course 2: *Healing Love: Seminal and Ovarian Kung Fu; Transforming Sexual Energy to Higher Centers, and the Art of Harmonious Relationships*

For more than five thousand years of Chinese history, the "no-outlet method" of retaining the seminal fluid during sexual union has remained a well-guarded secret. At first it was practiced exclusively by the Emperor and his innermost circle. Then, it passed from father to chosen son alone, excluding all female family members. Seminal and Ovarian Kung Fu practices teach men and women how to transform and circulate sexual energy through the Microcosmic Orbit. Rather than eliminating sexual intercourse, ancient Taoist yogis learned how to utilize sexual energy as a means of enhancing their internal practice.

The conservation and transformation of sexual energy during intercourse acts as a revitalizing factor in the physical and spiritual development of both men and women. The turning back and circulating of the generative force from the sexual organs to the higher energy centers of the body invigorates and rejuvenates all the vital functions. Mastering this practice produces a deep sense of respect for all forms of life.

In ordinary sexual union, the partners usually experience a type of orgasm which is limited to the genital area. Through special Taoist techniques, men and women learn to experience a total body orgasm without indiscriminate loss of vital energy. The conservation and transformation of sexual energy is essential for the work required in advanced Taoist practice.

Seminal and Ovarian Kung Fu is one of the five main branches of Taoist Esoteric Yoga.

Course 3: *Iron Shirt Chi Kung; Organs Exercises and Preliminary Rooting Principle*

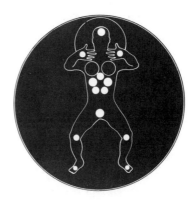

The Iron Shirt practice is divided into three parts: Iron Shirt I, II, and III.

The physical integrity of the body is sustained and protected through the accumulation and circulation of internal power (Chi) in the vital organs. The Chi energy that began to circulate freely through the Microcosmic Orbit and later the Fusion practices can be stored in the fasciae as well as in the vital organs. Fasciae are layers of connective tissues covering, supporting, or connecting the organs and muscles.

The purpose of storing Chi in the organs and muscles is to create a protective layer of interior power that enables the body to withstand unexpected injuries. Iron Shirt training roots the body to the Earth, strengthens the vital organs, changes the tendons, cleanses the bone marrow, and creates a reserve of pure Chi energy.

Iron Shirt Chi Kung is one of the foundations of spiritual practices since it provides a firm rooting for the ascension of the spirit body. The higher the spirit goes, the more solid its rooting to the Earth must be.

Iron Shirt Chi Kung I—Connective Tissues' and Organs' Exercise: On the first level of Iron Shirt, by using certain standing postures, muscle locks, and Iron Shirt Chi Kung breathing techniques, one learns how to draw and circulate energy from the ground. The standing postures teach how to connect the internal structure (bones, muscles, tendons, and fasciae) with the ground so that rooting power is developed. Through breathing techniques, internal power is directed to the organs, the twelve tendon channels, and the fasciae.

Over time, Iron Shirt strengthens the vital organs as well as the tendons, muscles, bones, and marrow. As the internal structure is strengthened through layers of Chi energy, the problems of poor posture and circulation of energy are corrected. The practitioner learns the importance of being physically and psychologically rooted in the Earth, a vital factor in the more advanced stages of Taoist practice.

Iron Shirt Chi Kung II — Tendons' Exercise: In the second level of Iron Shirt, one learns how to combine the mind, heart, bone structure, and Chi flow into one moving unit. The static forms learned in the first level of Iron Shirt evolve at this level into moving postures. The goal of Iron Shirt II is to develop rooting power and the ability to absorb and discharge energy through the tendons. A series of exercises allow the student to change, grow, and strengthen the tendons, to stimulate the vital organs, and to integrate the fasciae, tendons, bones, and muscles into one piece. The student also learns methods for releasing accumulated toxins in the muscles and joints of the body. Once energy flows freely through the organs, accumulated poisons can be discharged out of the body very efficiently without resorting to extreme fasts or special dietary aids.

Iron Shirt Chi Kung I is a prerequisite for this course.

Bone Marrow Nei Kung (Iron Shirt Chi Kung III) — Cleansing the Marrow: In the third level of Iron Shirt, one learns how to cleanse and grow the bone marrow, regenerate sexual hormones and store them in the fasciae, tendons, and marrow, as well as how to direct the internal power to the higher energy centers.

This level of Iron Shirt works directly on the organs, bones, and tendons in order to strengthen the entire system beyond its ordinary capacity. An extremely efficient method of vibrating the internal organs allows the practitioner to shake toxic deposits out of the inner structure of each organ by enhancing Chi circulation. This once highly secret method of advanced Iron Shirt, also known as the Golden Bell System, draws the energy produced in the sexual organs into the higher energy centers to carry out advanced Taoist practices.

Iron Shirt Chi Kung is one of the five essential branches of Taoist Esoteric Practice.

Prior study of Iron Shirt Chi Kung I and Healing Love are prerequisites for this course.

Course 4: *Fusion of the Five Elements,*
Cleansing of the Organs, and
Opening of the Six Special Channels

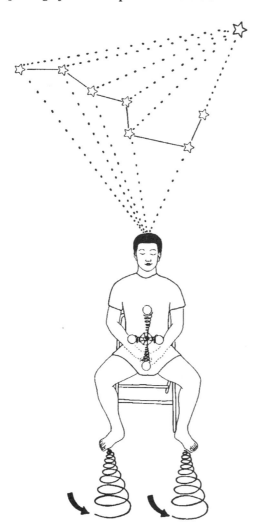

Fusion of the Five Elements and Cleansing of the Organs I, II, and III is the second formula of the Taoist Yoga Meditation of Internal Alchemy. At this level, one learns how the five elements (Earth, Metal, Fire, Wood, and Water), and their corresponding organs (spleen, lungs, heart, liver, and kidneys) interact with one another in three distinct ways: producing, combining, and strengthening. The Fusion practice combines the energies of the five elements and their corresponding emotions into one harmonious whole.

Fusion of the Five Elements I: In this practice of internal alchemy, the student learns to transform the negative emotions of worry, sadness, cruelty, anger, and fear into pure energy. This process is accomplished by identifying the source of the negative emotions within the five organs of the body. After the excessive energy of the emotions is filtered out of the organs, the state of psycho/physical balance is restored to the body. Freed of negative emotions, the pure energy of the five organs is crystallized into a radiant pearl or crystal ball. The pearl is circulated in the body and attracts to it energy from external sources — Universal Energy, Cosmic Particle Energy, and Earth Energy. The pearl plays a central role in the development and nourishment of the soul or energy body. The energy body then is nourished with the pure (virtue) energy of the five organs.

Fusion of the Five Elements II: The second level of Fusion practice teaches additional methods of circulating the pure energy of the five organs once they are freed of negative emotions. When the five organs are cleansed, the positive emotions of kindness, gentleness, respect, fairness, justice, and compassion rise as a natural expression of internal balance. The practitioner is able to monitor his state of balance by observing the quality of emotions arising spontaneously within.

The energy of the positive emotions is used to open the three channels running from the perineum, at the base of the sexual organs, to the top of the head. These channels collectively are known as the Thrusting Channels or Routes. In addition, a series of nine levels called the Belt Channel is opened, encircling the nine major energy centers of the body.

Fusion of Five Elements III: The third level of Fusion practice completes the cleansing of the energy channels in the body by opening the positive and negative leg and arm channels. The opening of the Microcosmic Orbit, the Thrusting Channels, the Belt Channel, the Great Regulator, and Great Bridge Channels makes the body extremely permeable to the circulation of vital energy. The unhindered circulation of energy is the foundation of perfect physical and emotional health.

The Fusion practice is one of the greatest achievements of the ancient

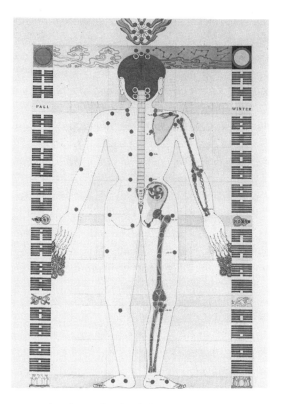

Taoist masters, as it gives the individual a way of freeing the body of negative emotions, and, at the same time, allows the pure virtues to shine forth.

Course 5: *Tai Chi Chi Kung;*
The Foundation
of Tai Chi Chuan

The Tai Chi practice is divided into seven workshops: (1) the Original Thirteen Movements' Form (five directions, eight movements); (2) Fast Form of Discharging Energy; (3) Long Form (108 movements); (4) Tai Chi Sword; (5) Tai Chi Knife; (6) Tai Chi Short and Long Stick; (7) Self-Defense Applications and Mat Work.

Through Tai Chi Chuan the practitioner learns to move the body in one unit, utilizing Chi energy rather than muscle power. Without the circulation of Chi through the channels, muscles, and tendons, the Tai Chi Chuan movements are only physical exercises with little effect on the inner structure of the body. In the practice of Tai Chi Chi Kung, the increased energy flow developed through the Microcosmic Orbit, Fusion work, and Iron Shirt practice is integrated into ordinary movement, so that the body learns more efficient ways of utilizing energy in motion. Improper body movements restrict energy flow causing energy blockages, poor posture, and, in some cases, serious illness. Quite often, back problems are the result of improper posture, accumulated tension, weakened bone structure, and psychological stress.

Through Tai Chi one learns how to use one's own mass as a power to work along with the force of gravity rather than against it. A result of increased body awareness through movement is an increased awareness of one's environment and the potentials it contains. The Tai Chi practitioner may utilize the integrated movements of the body as a means of self-defense in negative situations. Since Tai Chi is a gentle way of exercising and keeping the body fit, it can be practiced well into advanced age because the movements do not strain one's physical capacity as some aerobic exercises do.

Before beginning to study the Tai Chi Chuan form, the student must complete: (1) Opening of the Microcosmic Orbit, (2) Seminal and Ovarian Kung Fu, (3) Iron Shirt Chi Kung I, and (4) Tai Chi Chi Kung.

Tai Chi Chi Kung is divided into seven levels.

Tai Chi Chi Kung I is comprised of four parts:

a. Mind: (1) How to use one's own mass together with the force of gravity; (2) how to use the bone structure to move the whole body with very little muscular effort; and (3) how to learn and master the thirteen movements so that the mind can concentrate on directing the Chi energy.

b. Mind and Chi: Use the mind to direct the Chi flow.

c. Mind, Chi, and Earth force: How to integrate the three forces into one unit moving unimpeded through the bone structure.

d. Learn applications of Tai Chi for self-defense.

Tai Chi Chi Kung II—Fast Form of Discharging Energy:

a. Learn how to move fast in the five directions.

b. Learn how to move the entire body structure as one piece.

c. Discharge the energy from the Earth through the body structure.

Tai Chi Chi Kung III—Long Form Tai Chi Chuan:

a. Learn the 108 movements form.
b. Learn how to bring Chi into each movement.
c. Learn the second level of self-defense.
d. Grow "Chi eyes."
Tai Chi Chi Kung IV—the Tai Chi Sword.
Tai Chi Chi Kung V—Tai Chi Knife.
Tai Chi Chi Kung VI—Tai Chi Short and Long Stick.
Tai Chi Chi Kung VII—Application of Self-Defense and Mat Work.
Tai Chi Chuan is one of the five essential branches of the Taoist practice.

Course 6: *Taoist Five Element Nutrition; Taoist Healing Diet*
Proper diet in tune with one's body needs, and an awareness of the seasons and the climate we live in are integral parts of the Healing Tao. It is not enough to eat healthy foods free of chemical pollutants to have good health. One has to learn the proper combination of foods according to the five tastes and the five element theory. By knowing one's predominant element, one can learn how to counteract imbalances inherent in one's nature. Also, as the seasons change, dietary needs vary. One must know how to adjust them to fit one's level of activity. Proper diet can become an instrument for maintaining health and cultivating increased levels of awareness.

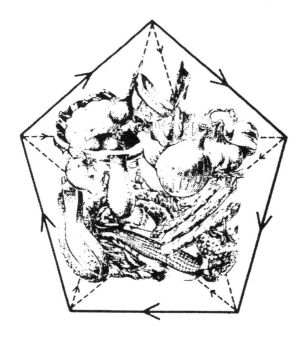

INTRODUCTORY LEVEL III: The Way of Radiant Health

Course 7: *Healing Hands Kung Fu; Awaken the Healing Hand – Five Finger Kung Fu*

The ability to heal oneself and others is one of the five essential branches of the Healing Tao practice. Five Finger Kung Fu integrates both static and dynamic exercise forms in order to cultivate and nourish Chi which accumulates in the organs, penetrates the fasciae, tendons, and muscles, and is finally transferred out through the hands and fingers. Practitioners of body-centered therapies and various healing arts will benefit from this technique. Through the practice of Five Finger Kung Fu, you will learn how to expand your breathing capacity in order to further strengthen your internal organs, tone and stretch the lower back and abdominal muscles, regulate weight, and connect with Father Heaven and Mother Earth healing energy; and you will learn how to develop the ability to concentrate for self-healing.

Course 8: *Chi Nei Tsang; Organ Chi Transformation Massage*

The practice is divided into three levels: Chi Nei Tsang I, II, and III.

Chi Nei Tsang, or Organ Chi Transformation Massage, is an entire system of Chinese deep healing that works with the energy flow of the five major systems in the body: the vascular system, the lymphatic system, the nervous system, the tendon/muscle system, and the acupuncture meridian system.

In the Chi Nei Tsang practice, one is able to increase energy flow to specific organs through massaging a series of points in the navel area. In Taoist practice, it is believed that all the Chi energy and the organs, glands, brain, and nervous system are joined in the navel; therefore, energy blockages in the navel area often manifest as symptoms in other parts of the body. The abdominal cavity contains the large intestine, small intestine, liver, gall bladder, stomach, spleen, pancreas, bladder, and sex organs, as well as many lymph nodes. The aorta and vena cava divide into two branches at the navel area, descending into the legs.

Chi Nei Tsang works on the energy blockages in the navel and then follows the energy into the other parts of the body. Chi Nei Tsang is a very deep science of healing brought to the United States by Master Mantak Chia.

Course 9: *Space Dynamics; The Taoist Art of Placement*
Feng Shui has been used by Chinese people and emperors for five thousand years. It combines ancient Chinese Geomancy, Taoist Metaphysics, dynamic Psychology, and modern Geomagnetics to diagnose energy, power, and phenomena in nature, people, and buildings. The student will gain greater awareness of his own present situation, and see more choices for freedom and growth through the interaction of the Five Elements.

INTERMEDIATE LEVEL: Foundations of Spiritual Practice

Course 10: *Lesser Enlightenment (Kan and Li); Opening of the Twelve Channels; Raising the Soul andDeveloping theEnergy Body*

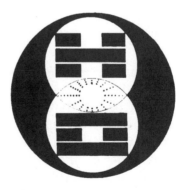

Lesser Enlightenment of Kan and Li (Yin and Yang Mixed): This formula is called *Siaow Kan Li* in Chinese, and involves a literal steaming of the sexual energy (Ching or creative) into life-force energy (Chi) in order to feed the soul or energy body. One might say that the transfer of the sexual energy power throughout the whole body and brain begins with the practice of Kan and Li. The crucial secret of this formula is to reverse the usual sites of Yin and Yang power, thereby provoking liberation of the sexual energy.

This formula includes the cultivation of the root (the Hui-Yin) and the heart center, and the transformation of sexual energy into pure Chi at the navel. This inversion places the heat of the bodily fire beneath the coolness of the bodily water. Unless this inversion takes place, the fire simply moves up and burns the body out. The water (the sexual fluid) has the tendency to flow downward and out. When it dries out, it is the end. This formula reverses normal wasting of energy by the highly advanced method of placing the water in a closed vessel (cauldron) in the body, and then cooking the sperm (sexual energy) with the fire beneath. If the water (sexual energy) is not sealed, it will flow directly into the fire and extinguish it or itself be consumed.

This formula preserves the integrity of both elements, thus allowing the steaming to go on for great periods of time. The essential formula is to never let the fire rise without having water to heat above it, and to never allow the water to spill into the fire. Thus, a warm, moist steam is produced containing tremendous energy and health benefits, to regrow all the glands, the nervous system, and the lymphatic system, and to increase pulsation.

The formula consists of:

1. Mixing the water (Yin) and fire (Yang), or male and female, to give birth to the soul;
2. Transforming the sexual power (creative force) into vital energy (Chi), gathering and purifying the Microcosmic outer alchemical agent;
3. Opening the twelve major channels;
4. Circulating the power in the solar orbit (cosmic orbit);
5. Turning back the flow of generative force to fortify the body and the brain, and restore it to its original condition before puberty;
6. Regrowing the thymus gland and lymphatic system;
7. Sublimation of the body and soul: self-intercourse. Giving birth to the immortal soul (energy body).

Course 11: *Greater Enlightenment (Kan and Li); Raising the Spirit and Developing the Spiritual Body*

This formula comprises the Taoist Dah Kan Li (Ta Kan Li) practice. It uses the same energy relationship of Yin and Yang inversion but increases to an extraordinary degree the amount of energy that may be drawn up into the body. At this stage, the mixing, transforming, and harmonizing of energy takes place in the solar plexus. The increasing amplitude of power is due to the fact that the formula not only draws Yin and Yang energy from within the body, but also draws the power directly from Heaven and Earth or ground (Yang and Yin, respectively), and adds the elemental powers to those of one's own body. In fact, power can be drawn from any energy source, such as the Moon, wood, Earth, flowers, animals, light, etc.

The formula consists of:

1. Moving the stove and changing the cauldron;
2. Greater water and fire mixture (self-intercourse);
3. Greater transformation of sexual power into the higher level;
4. Gathering the outer and inner alchemical agents to restore the generative force and invigorate the brain;
5. Cultivating the body and soul;
6. Beginning the refining of the sexual power (generative force, vital force, Ching Chi);
7. Absorbing Mother Earth (Yin) power and Father Heaven (Yang) power. Mixing with sperm and ovary power (body), and soul;
8. Raising the soul;
9. Retaining the positive generative force (creative) force, and keeping it from draining away;
10. Gradually doing away with food, and depending on self sufficiency and universal energy;
11. Giving birth to the spirit, transferring good virtues and Chi energy channels into the spiritual body;
12. Practicing to overcome death;
13. Opening the crown;
14. Space travelling.

Course 12: *Greatest Enlightenment (Kan and Li)*

This formula is Yin and Yang power mixed at a higher energy center. It helps to reverse the aging process by re-establishing the thymus glands and increasing natural immunity. This means that healing energy is radiated from a more powerful point in the body, providing greater benefits to the physical and ethereal bodies.

The formula consists of:

1. Moving the stove and changing the cauldron to the higher center;
2. Absorbing the Solar and Lunar power;

3. Greatest mixing, transforming, steaming, and purifying of sexual power (generative force), soul, Mother Earth, Father Heaven, Solar and Lunar power for gathering the Microcosmic inner alchemical agent;
4. Mixing the visual power with the vital power;
5. Mixing (sublimating) the body, soul and spirit.

ADVANCED LEVEL: The Realm of Soul and Spirit

Course 13: *Sealing of the Five Senses*
This very high formula effects a literal transmutation of the warm current or Chi into mental energy or energy of the soul. To do this, we must seal the five senses, for each one is an open gate of energy loss. In other words, power flows out from each of the sense organs unless there is an esoteric sealing of these doors of energy movement. They must release energy only when specifically called upon to convey information.

Abuse of the senses leads to far more energy loss and degradation than people ordinarily realize. Examples of misuse of the senses are as follows: if you look too much, the seminal fluid is harmed; listen too much, and the mind is harmed; speak too much, and the salivary glands are harmed; cry too much, and the blood is harmed; have sexual intercourse too often, and the marrow is harmed, etc.

Each of the elements has a corresponding sense through which its elemental force may be gathered or spent. The eye corresponds to fire; the tongue to water; the left ear to metal; the right ear to wood; the nose to Earth.

The fifth formula consists of:
1. Sealing the five thieves: ears, eyes, nose, tongue, and body;
2. Controlling the heart, and seven emotions (pleasure, anger, sorrow, joy, love, hate, and desire);
3. Uniting and transmuting the inner alchemical agent into life-preserving true vitality;
4. Purifying the spirit;
5. Raising and educating the spirit; stopping the spirit from wandering outside in quest of sense data;
6. Eliminating decayed food, depending on the undecayed food, the universal energy is the True Breatharian.

Course 14: *Congress of Heaven and Earth*
This formula is difficult to describe in words. It involves the incarna-

tion of a male and a female entity within the body of the adept. These two entities have sexual intercourse within the body. It involves the mixing of the Yin and Yang powers on and about the crown of the head, being totally open to receive energy from above, and the regrowth of the pineal gland to its fullest use. When the pineal gland has developed to its fullest potential, it will serve as a compass to tell us in which direction our aspirations can be found. Taoist Esotericism is a method of mastering the spirit, as described in Taoist Yoga. Without the body, the Tao cannot be attained, but with the body, truth can never be realized. The practitioner of Taoism should preserve his physical body with the same care as he would a precious diamond, because it can be used as a medium to achieve immortality. If, however, you do not abandon it when you reach your destination, you will not realize the truth.

This formula consists of:
1. Mingling (uniting) the body, soul, spirit, and the universe (cosmic orbit);
2. Fully developing the positive to eradicate the negative completely;
3. Returning the spirit to nothingness.

Course 15: *Reunion of Heaven and Man*

We compare the body to a ship, and the soul to the engine and propeller of a ship. This ship carries a very precious and very large diamond which it is assigned to transport to a very distant shore. If your ship is damaged (a sick and ill body), no matter how good the engine is, you are not going to get very far and may even sink. Thus, we advise against spiritual training unless all of the channels in the body have been properly opened, and have been made ready to receive the 10,000 or 100,000 volts of super power which will pour down into them. The Taoist approach, which has been passed down to us for over five thousand years, consists of many thousands of methods. The formulae and practices we describe in these books are based on such secret knowledge and the author's own experience during over twenty years of study and of successively teaching thousands of students.

The main goal of Taoists:
1. This level — overcoming reincarnation, and the fear of death through enlightenment;
2. Higher level — the immortal spirit and life after death;
3. Highest level — the immortal spirit in an immortal body. This body functions like a mobile home to the spirit and soul as it moves through the subtle planes, allowing greater power of manifestation.

Healing Tao Books

AWAKEN HEALING ENER-GY THROUGH THE TAO

This book reveals for the first time in vivid detail the essentials of the Microcosmic Orbit meditation, a way to awaken your own healing energy. Learn how to strengthen your internal organs and increase circulation through the flow of Chi energy. Included are precise instructions for practice, and detailed illustrations of energy centers, organs, and anatomical structures as well as descriptions of the higher levels of the Taoist meditation system. By Master Mantak Chia. Softbound. 193 pages.

$10.95, plus $1.95 for postage and handling
Order by Item No. B01

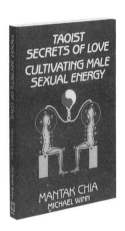

TAOIST SECRETS OF LOVE: CULTIVATING MALE SEXUAL ENERGY

Master Mantak Chia reveals for the first time to the general public the ancient sexual secrets of the Taoist sages. These methods enable men to conserve and transform sexual energy through its circulation in the Microcosmic Orbit, invigorating and rejuvenating the body's vital functions. Hidden for centuries, these esoteric techniques make the process of linking sexual energy and transcendent states of consciousness accessible to the reader.

This revolutionary book teaches:

- Higher Taoist practices for alchemical transmutation of body, mind, and spirit;
- The secret of achieving and maintaining full sexual potency;
- The Taoist "valley orgasm" — pathway to higher bliss;
- How to conserve and store sperm in the body;
- The exchange and balancing of male and female energies within the body, and with one's partner;
- How this can fuel higher achievement in career, personal power, and sports.

This book, co-authored with Michael Winn, is written clearly, and illustrated with many detailed diagrams. Softbound. 250 pages.

$14.00, plus $1.95 for postage and handling
Order by Item No. B02

HEALING LOVE THROUGH THE TAO: CULTIVATING FEMALE SEXUAL ENERGY

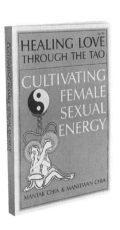

This book outlines the methods for cultivating female sexual energy. Master Mantak Chia and Maneewan Chia introduce for the first time in the West the different techniques for transforming and circulating female sexual energy. The book teaches:

- The Taoist internal alchemical practices to nourish body, mind, and spirit;
- How to eliminate energy loss through menstruation;
- How to reduce the length of menstruations;
- How to conserve and store ovary energy in the body;
- The exchange and balance of male and female energies within the body, and with one's partner;
- How to rejuvenate the body and mind through vaginal exercises.

Written in clear language by Master Mantak Chia and Maneewan Chia. Published by Healing Tao Books. Softbound. 328 pages.

$14.95, plus $1.95 for postage and handling
Order by Item No. B06

TAOIST WAYS TO TRANSFORM STRESS INTO VITALITY

The foundations of success, personal power, health, and peak performance are created by knowing how to transform stress into vitality and power using the techniques of the Inner Smile and Six Healing Sounds, and circulating the smile energy in the Microcosmic Orbit.

The Inner Smile teaches you how to connect with your inner organs, fall in love with them, and smile to them, so that the emotions and stress can be transformed into creativity, learning, healing, and peak performance energy.

The Six Healing Sounds help to cool down the system, eliminate trapped energy, and clean the toxins out of the organs to establish organs that are in peak condition.

By Master Mantak Chia. Published by Healing Tao Books. Softbound. 156 pages.

$10.95, plus $1.95 for postage and handling
Order by Item No. B03

CHI SELF-MASSAGE: THE TAOIST WAY OF REJUVENATION

Tao Rejuvenation uses one's internal energy or Chi to strengthen and rejuvenate the sense organs (eyes, ears, nose, tongue), the teeth, the skin, and the inner organs. The techniques are five thousand years old, and, until now, were closely guarded secrets passed on from a Master to a small group of students, with each Master only knowing a small part. For the first time the entire system has been pieced together in a logical sequence, and is presented in such a way that only five or ten minutes of practice daily will improve complexion, vision, hearing, sinuses, gums, teeth, tongue, internal organs, and general stamina. (This form of massage is very different from muscular massage.)

By Master Mantak Chia. Published by Healing Tao Books. Softbound. 176 pages.

$10.95, plus $1.95 for postage and handling
Order by Item No. B04

IRON SHIRT CHI KUNG I: INTERNAL ORGANS EXERCISE

The main purpose of Iron Shirt is not for fighting, but to perfect the body, to win great health, to increase performance, to fight disease, to protect the vital organs from injuries, and to lay the groundwork for higher, spiritual work. Iron Shirt I teaches how to increase the performance of the organs during sports, speech, singing, and dancing.

Learn how to increase the Chi pressure throughout the whole system by Iron Shirt Chi Kung breathing, to awaken and circulate internal energy (Chi), to transfer force through the bone structure and down to the ground. Learn how to direct the Earth's power through your bone structure, to direct the internal power to energize and strengthen the organs, and to energize and increase the Chi pressure in the fasciae (connective tissues).

By Master Mantak Chia. Published by Healing Tao Books. Softbound. 320 pages.

$14.95, plus $1.95 for postage and handling
Order by Item No. B05

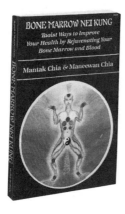

BONE MARROW NEI KUNG: IRON SHIRT CHI KUNG III

Bone Marrow Nei Kung is a system to cultivate internal power. By absorbing cosmic energy into the bones, the bone marrow is revitalized, blood replenished, and the life-force within is nourished. These methods are known to make the body impervious to illness and disease. In ancient times, the "Steel Body" attained through this practice was a coveted asset in the fields of Chinese medicine and martial arts. Taoist methods of "regrowing" the bone marrow are crucial to rejuvenating the body, which in turn rejuvenates the mind and spirit. This system has not been revealed before, but in this ground-breaking work Master Mantak Chia divulges the step-by-step practice of his predecessors.

By Master Mantak Chia and Maneewan Chia. Published by Healing Tao Books. Softbound. 288 pages.

$14.95, plus $1.95 for postage and handling
Order by Item No. B08

FUSION OF THE FIVE ELEMENTS I

Fusion of the Five Elements I, first in the Taoist Inner Alchemy Series, offers basic and advanced meditations for transforming negative emotions. Based on the Taoist Five Element Theory regarding the five elemental forces of the universe, the student learns how to control negative energies and how to transform them into useful energy. The student also learns how to create a pearl of radiant energy and how to increase its power with additional internal energy (virtue energy) as well as external sources of energy —

Universal, Cosmic Particle, and Earth. All combine in a balanced way to prepare the pearl for its use in the creation of an energy body. The creation of the energy body is the next major step in achieving the goal of creating an immortal spirit. Master Mantak Chia leads you, step by step, into becoming an emotionally balanced, controlled, and stronger individual as he offers you the key to a spiritual independence.

By Master Mantak Chia and Maneewan Chia. Published by Healing Tao Books. Softbound. 199 pages.

$12.95, plus $1.95 for postage and handling
Order by Item No. B09

FORTHCOMING PUBLICATIONS

- **Chi Nei Tsang** — Organ Chi transformation through a precise procedure of massage.
- **The Healing Light** — The foundation meditation practice of the Healing Tao System for channeling energy and self-empowerment.
- **Tai Chi Chi Kung I** — The inner structure of Tai Chi.
- **Five Element Nutrition** — Ancient Chinese cooking based on the Five Elements Theory.
- **Fusion of the Five Elements II** — Thrusting and Belt Channels. Growing positive emotions, psychic and emotional self-defense.

HEALING TAO JOURNAL

The new *Healing Tao Journal* contains questions and answers with Master Chia, notices of new books, case histories of Taoist practice, interviews, Taoist Five Element Nutrition recipes, and much more of interest. The *Healing Tao Journal* is the best way to keep up-to-date with the Healing Tao practice in its many applications.

$10.00 for a one-year subscription (2 copies)
$18.00 for a two-year subscription (4 copies)

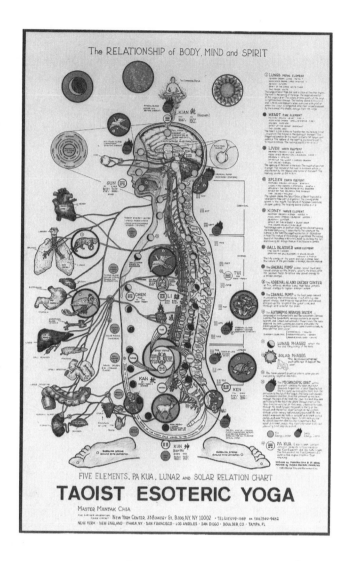

TAO BODY/MIND/SPIRIT CHART
23" × 35", full-color chart by Susan McKay. Illustrates the organs, their associations, and Healing Sounds; points on the Microcosmic Orbit and their associations; the body and its five elements, eight-trigram, lunar and solar correspondences; centers of higher-level practices; and the development of the spirit.

$7.50 per copy, plus $1.95 postage and handling.
Order by Item No. CH47

POSTERS

18 × 22", four-color process posters were created by artist Juan Li. Please order by item number.

**$7.50 per poster, plus $1.95 for postage and handling.
On orders of three or more posters, $3.60 postage and handling.
$95.00 per set of fourteen posters, free postage and handling.
OrderbyItem No. 45.**

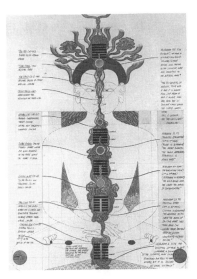

The Microcosmic Orbit — Small Heavenly Cycle — The Functional Channel (Yin). The Microcosmic Orbit Meditation is the key to circulating internal healing energy, and is the gateway to higher Taoist Meditations. **Item No. P31**

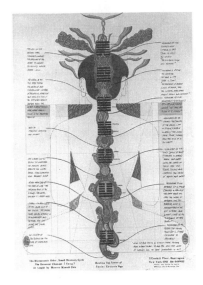

The Microcosmic Orbit — Small Heavenly Cycle — The Governor Channel (Yang). The Governor Channel of the Microcosmic Orbit Meditation allows the Yang (hot) energy to flow from the base of the spine to the brain. **Item No. P32**

The Six Healing Sounds. The Six Healing Sounds dispel illness, relieve stress, and cool over-heated emotions. **Item No. P33**

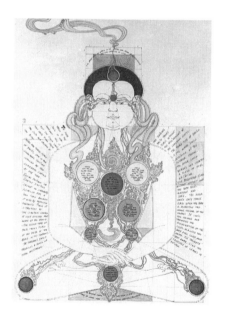

The Secret of the Inner Smile. The Inner Smile is the secret for living in simple harmony with yourself and others. The Inner Smile is the smile of total happiness. This is not the social smile. This smile rises from the cells and organs of the body. **Item No. P34**

Healing Love and Sex—Seminal Kung Fu. By conserving their seeds during lovemaking, men can transform sexual energy into spiritual love, and, at the same time, enjoy a higher orgasm. The main purpose of Seminal and Ovarian Kung Fu is to utilize sexual energy for attaining higher levels of consciousness so that the sexual urge does not control the person. **Item No. P35**

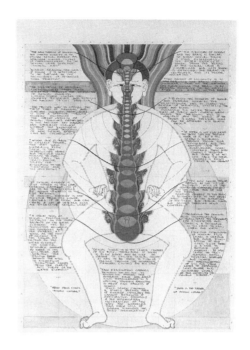

Healing Love and Sex—Ovarian Kung Fu. The Taoists teach women to regulate their menstrual flow and transmute sexual orgasm into higher spiritual love. The techniques of Seminal and Ovarian Kung Fu allow the practitioner to harness sexual impulses so that sex does not control the person. By controlling sexual impulses, people are able to move from the mortal level into higher levels of consciousness. **Item No. P36**

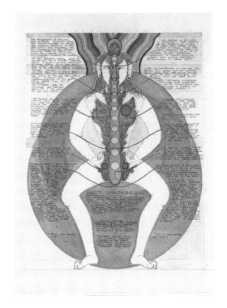

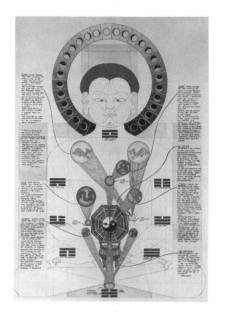

Fusion of the Five Elements I – Cleansing, Clearing, and Harmonizing of the Organs and the Emotions. Each organ stores a separate emotional energy. When fused into a single balanced Chi at the navel, the opening of the six special channels becomes possible. **Item No. P37**

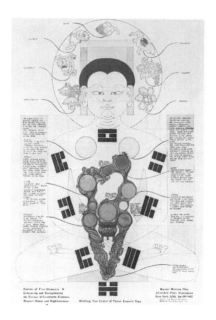

Fusion of the Five Elements II – Enhancing and Strengthening the Virtues. Fusion of the Five Elements II strengthens positive emotions, balances the organs, and encourages in men and women the natural virtues of gentleness, kindness, respect, honor, and righteousness. **Item No. P38**

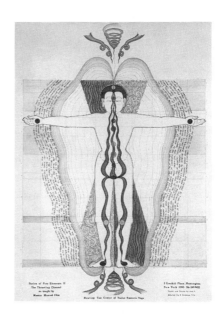

Fusion of the Five Elements II — Thrusting Channels. Running through the center of the body, the Thrusting Routes allow the absorption of cosmic energies for greater radiance and power. **Item No. P39**

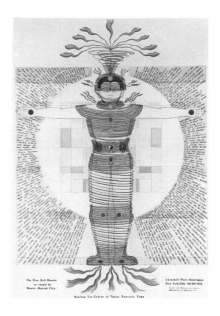

Fusion of the Five Elements II — Nine Belt Channel. The Taoist Belt Channel spins a web of Chi around the major energy vortexes in the body, protecting the psyche by connecting the power of Heaven and Earth. **Item No. P40**

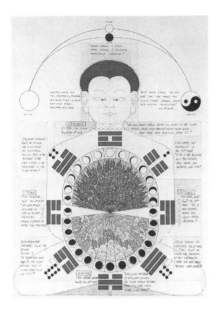

The Harmony of Yin and Yang. "Yin cannot function without the help of Yang; Yang cannot function without the help of Yin." — Taoist Canon, 8th century A.D. **Item No. P41**

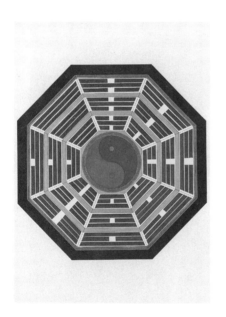

Pa Kua. The Cauldron of Fusing the Energy and Emotions. **Item No. P42**

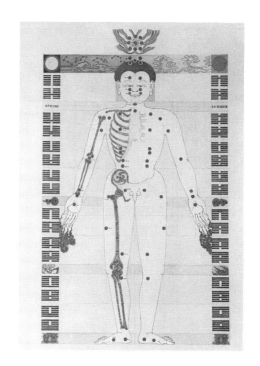

Fusion of the Five Elements III—Yin Bridge and Regulator Channels. Fusion of the Five Elements III uses special meridians to cleanse the aura and regulate high-voltage energy absorbed by the body during meditation. **Item No. P43**

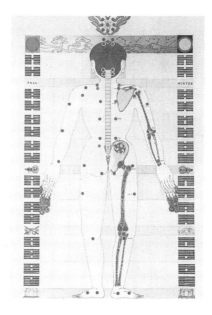

Fusion of the Five Elements III—Yang Bridge and Regulator Channels. Fusion of the Five Elements III teaches the yogic secrets of safely regulating the release of the kundalini power using special meridians. **Item No. P44**

VHS VIDEOS

Invite Master Chia into your living room.

$55.00 per tape. Please order by Item Number. Our videos are not compatible with the PAL System. **Add postage and handling as follows: 1 video—$3.00, 2 videos—$4.75, 3 or more videos—$5.50.**

Guided Practice

Item	Title
V50	Tai Chi Chi Kung I
V51	Tai Chi Chi Kung II
V58	Iron Shirt Chi Kung III
V60	Healing Hand/Buddha Palm

Weekend Workshops

Item	Title
V57-TP	Iron Shirt Chi Kung I / Theory and Practice
V61-T	Microcosmic Orbit / Theory
V61-M	Microcosmic Orbit / Meditation
V62-TP	Six Healing Sounds / Theory and Practice
V63-T	Healing Love through The Tao / Theory
V63-P	Healing Love through The Tao / Practice
V64-T	Fusion of Five Elements I / Theory
V64-M	Fusion of Five Elements I / Meditation
V65-T	Fusion of Five Elements II / Theory
V65-M	Fusion of Five Elements II / Meditation
V66-T	Fusion of Five Elements III / Theory
V66-M	Fusion of Five Elements III / Meditation

CASSETTE TAPES

Guided Practice
Tapes C09-C18 are guided by Master Mantak Chia.

Item No.	Title	No. of Tapes	Price	Postage & Handling
C09	Inner Smile	1	$ 9.95	$ 1.95
C10	Six Healing Sounds	1	9.95	1.95
C11	Microcosmic Orbit	1	9.95	1.95
C11a	Healing Love	1	9.95	1.95
C12	Tai Chi Chi Kung I	1	9.95	1.95
C13	Iron Shirt Chi Kung I	1	9.95	1.95
C16	Fusion of the Five Elements I	1	9.95	1.95
C17	Fusion of the Five Elements II	1	9.95	1.95
C18	Fusion of the Five Elements III	1	9.95	1.95

Weekend Workshops
Taught by Master Mantak Chia.

Item No.	Title	No. of Tapes	Price	Postage & Handling
C19	Microcosmic Orbit: complete the Microcosmic Orbit, Six Healing Sounds, Inner Smile	6	$ 42.00	$ 7.75
C20	Tai Chi Chi Kung I	4	30.00	6.95
C21	Iron Shirt Chi Kung I	4	30.00	6.95
C23	Iron Shirt Chi Kung III	4	30.00	6.95
C24	Fusion of the Five Elements I	4	30.00	6.95
C25	Fusion of the Five Elements II	4	30.00	6.95
C26	Fusion of the Five Elements III	4	30.00	6.95
C27	Healing Love	4	30.00	6.95

Retreats (sold only in complete sets)

Item No.	Title	Price	Postage & Handling
C29	Lesser Kan and Li	$185.00	$14.50
C30	Greater Kan and Li	185.00	14.50
C31	Greatest Kan and Li	185.00	14.50

Catalog

BONE MARROW NEI KUNG (IRON SHIRT) EQUIPMENT

Item No.	Title	Price	Postage & Handling
62C	Untreated Drilled Jade Egg with Handbook	$15.95	$4.75
62D	Bar for the Chi Weight-Lifting Exercise	14.50	4.75
62E	Wire Hitter (for Bone Marrow Nei Kung)	15.00	4.75
62F	Rattan Hitter (for Bone Marrow Nei Kung)	14.00	3.00
62G	100% Silk Cloth for Chi Weight-Lifting and Massage	10.00	3.00
62H	Partial Set: Vaginal Chi Weight-Lifting Equipment Only (includes 62C, 62D, 62G)	39.95	7.75
62I	Set of Chi Weight-Lifting and Hitting Equipment for Women (includes 62C, 62D, 62E, 62F, 62G)	65.00	9.25
62J	Set of Chi Weight-Lifting and Hitting Equipment for Men (includes 62D, 62E, 62F, 62G)	50.00	8.50

THE INTERNATIONAL HEALING TAO CENTERS

For further information about any of our courses or centers, or to order books, posters, etc., please write or call:

The Healing Tao Center
P.O. Box 1194, Huntington, NY 11743
Phone: (516) 367-2701

There are also Healing Tao Centers in:

United States
Arizona
California
  Los Angeles
  San Francisco
Colorado
Connecticut
Delaware
Florida
Illinois
Indiana
Massachusetts
Michigan

Minnesota
New Jersey
New York
North Carolina
Oklahoma
Pennsylvania
Washington
Wisconsin

Canada
Ontario
British Columbia
Quebec

Europe
England
France
Holland
Switzerland
West Germany
Italy

Australia

India

South America